BRITANNICA
Mathematics in Context

Measure for Measure

Britannica

ENCYCLOPÆDIA BRITANNICA EDUCATIONAL CORPORATION

Mathematics in Context is a comprehensive middle grades curriculum. It was developed in collaboration with the Wisconsin Center for Education Research, School of Education, University of Wisconsin–Madison and the Freudenthal Institute at the University of Utrecht, The Netherlands, with the support of National Science Foundation Grant No. 9054928.

National Science Foundation

Opinions expressed are those of the authors
and not necessarily those of the Foundation

ISBN 0-7826-1491-4
1 2 3 4 5 6 7 8 9 10   99 98 97

The *Mathematics in Context* Development Team

Mathematics in Context is a comprehensive middle grades curriculum. The National Science Foundation funded the National Center for Research in Mathematical Sciences Education at the University of Wisconsin–Madison to develop and field-test the materials from 1991 through 1996. The Freudenthal Institute at the University of Utrecht in The Netherlands is the main subcontractor responsible for the development of the student and assessment materials.

The initial version of *Measure for Measure* was developed by Koeno Gravemeijer and Nina Boswinkel. It was adapted for use in American schools by Margaret R. Meyer and Julia A. Shew.

National Center for Research in Mathematical Sciences Education Staff

Thomas A. Romberg
Director

Joan Daniels Pedro
Assistant to the Director

Gail Burrill
Coordinator
Field Test Materials

Margaret R. Meyer
Coordinator
Pilot Test Materials

Mary Ann Fix
Editorial Coordinator

Sherian Foster
Editorial Coordinator

James A. Middleton
Pilot Test Coordinator

Project Staff

Jonathan Brendefur
Laura J. Brinker
James Browne
Jack Burrill
Rose Byrd
Peter Christiansen
Barbara Clarke
Doug Clarke
Beth R. Cole

Fae Dremock
Jasmina Milinkovic
Margaret A. Pligge
Mary C. Shafer
Julia A. Shew
Aaron N. Simon
Marvin Smith
Stephanie Z. Smith
Mary S. Spence

Freudenthal Institute Staff

Jan de Lange
Director

Els Feijs
Coordinator

Martin van Reeuwijk
Coordinator

Project Staff

Mieke Abels
Nina Boswinkel
Frans van Galen
Koeno Gravemeijer
Marja van den Heuvel-Panhuizen
Jan Auke de Jong
Vincent Jonker
Ronald Keijzer

Martin Kindt
Jansie Niehaus
Nanda Querelle
Anton Roodhardt
Leen Streefland
Adri Treffers
Monica Wijers
Astrid de Wild

Acknowledgments

Several school districts used and evaluated one or more versions of the materials: Ames Community School District, Ames, Iowa; Parkway School District, Chesterfield, Missouri; Stoughton Area School District, Stoughton, Wisconsin; Madison Metropolitan School District, Madison, Wisconsin; Milwaukee Public Schools, Milwaukee, Wisconsin; and Dodgeville School District, Dodgeville, Wisconsin. Two sites were involved in staff development as well as formative evaluation of materials: Culver City, California, and Memphis, Tennessee. Two sites were developed through partnership with Encyclopædia Britannica Educational Corporation: Miami, Florida, and Puerto Rico. University Partnerships were developed with mathematics educators who worked with preservice teachers to familiarize them with the curriculum and to obtain their advice on the curriculum materials. The materials were also used at several other schools throughout the United States.

We at Encyclopædia Britannica Educational Corporation extend our thanks to all who had a part in making this program a success. Some of the participants instrumental in the program's development are as follows:

Allapattah Middle School
Miami, Florida
Nemtalla (Nikolai) Barakat

Ames Middle School
Ames, Iowa
Kathleen Coe
Judd Freeman
Gary W. Schnieder
Ronald H. Stromen
Lyn Terrill

Bellerive Elementary
Creve Coeur, Missouri
Judy Hetterscheidt
Donna Lohman
Gary Alan Nunn
Jakke Tchang

Brookline Public Schools
Brookline, Massachusetts
Rhonda K. Weinstein
Deborah Winkler

Cass Middle School
Milwaukee, Wisconsin
Tami Molenda
Kyle F. Witty

Central Middle School
Waukesha, Wisconsin
Nancy Reese

Craigmont Middle School
Memphis, Tennessee
Sharon G. Ritz
Mardest K. VanHooks

Crestwood Elementary
Madison, Wisconsin
Diane Hein
John Kalson

Culver City Middle School
Culver City, California
Marilyn Culbertson
Joel Evans
Joy Ellen Kitzmiller
Patricia R. O'Connor
Myrna Ann Perks, Ph.D.
David H. Sanchez
John Tobias
Kelley Wilcox

Cutler Ridge Middle School
Miami, Florida
Lorraine A. Valladares

Dodgeville Middle School
Dodgeville, Wisconsin
Jacqueline A. Kamps
Carol Wolf

Edwards Elementary
Ames, Iowa
Diana Schmidt

Fox Prairie Elementary
Stoughton, Wisconsin
Tony Hjelle

Grahamwood Elementary
Memphis, Tennessee
M. Lynn McGoff
Alberta Sullivan

Henry M. Flagler Elementary
Miami, Florida
Frances R. Harmon

Horning Middle School
Waukesha, Wisconsin
Connie J. Marose
Thomas F. Clark

Huegel Elementary
Madison, Wisconsin
Nancy Brill
Teri Hedges
Carol Murphy

Hutchison Middle School
Memphis, Tennessee
Maria M. Burke
Vicki Fisher
Nancy D. Robinson

Idlewild Elementary
Memphis, Tennessee
Linda Eller

Jefferson Elementary
Santa Ana, California
Lydia Romero-Cruz

Jefferson Middle School
Madison, Wisconsin
Jane A. Beebe
Catherine Buege
Linda Grimmer
John Grueneberg
Nancy Howard
Annette Porter
Stephen H. Sprague
Dan Takkunen
Michael J. Vena

Jesus Sanabria Cruz School
Yabucoa, Puerto Rico
Andreíta Santiago Serrano

John Muir Elementary School
Madison, Wisconsin
Julie D'Onofrio
Jane M. Allen-Jauch
Kent Wells

Kegonsa Elementary
Stoughton, Wisconsin
Mary Buchholz
Louisa Havlik
Joan Olsen
Dominic Weisse

Linwood Howe Elementary
Culver City, California
Sandra Checel
Ellen Thireos

Mitchell Elementary
Ames, Iowa
Henry Gray
Matt Ludwig

New School of Northern Virginia
Fairfax, Virginia
Denise Jones

Northwood Elementary
Ames, Iowa
Eleanor M. Thomas

Orchard Ridge Elementary
Madison, Wisconsin
Mary Paquette
Carrie Valentine

Parkway West Middle School
Chesterfield, Missouri
Elissa Aiken
Ann Brenner
Gail R. Smith

Ridgeway Elementary
Ridgeway, Wisconsin
Lois Powell
Florence M. Wasley

Roosevelt Elementary
Ames, Iowa
Linda A. Carver

Roosevelt Middle
Milwaukee, Wisconsin
Sandra Simmons

Ross Elementary
Creve Coeur, Missouri
Annette Isselhard
Sheldon B. Korklan
Victoria Linn
Kathy Stamer

St. Joseph's School
Dodgeville, Wisconsin
Rita Van Dyck
Sharon Wimer

St. Maarten Academy
St. Peters, St. Maarten, NA
Shareed Hussain

Sarah Scott Middle School
Milwaukee, Wisconsin
Kevin Haddon

Sawyer Elementary
Ames, Iowa
Karen Bush Hoiberg

Sennett Middle School
Madison, Wisconsin
Brenda Abitz
Lois Bell
Shawn M. Jacobs

Sholes Middle School
Milwaukee, Wisconsin
Chris Gardner
Ken Haddon

Stephens Elementary
Madison, Wisconsin
Katherine Hogan
Shirley M. Steinbach
Kathleen H. Vegter

Stoughton Middle School
Stoughton, Wisconsin
Sally Bertelson
Polly Goepfert
Jacqueline M. Harris
Penny Vodak

Toki Middle School
Madison, Wisconsin
Gail J. Anderson
Vicky Grice
Mary M. Ihlenfeldt
Steve Jernegan
Jim Leidel
Theresa Loehr
Maryann Stephenson
Barbara Takkunen
Carol Welsch

Trowbridge Elementary
Milwaukee, Wisconsin
Jacqueline A. Nowak

W. R. Thomas Middle School
Miami, Florida
Michael Paloger

Wooddale Elementary Middle School
Memphis, Tennessee
Velma Quinn Hodges
Jacqueline Marie Hunt

Yahara Elementary
Stoughton, Wisconsin
Mary Bennett
Kevin Wright

Site Coordinators

Mary L. Delagardelle—Ames Community Schools, Ames, Iowa

Dr. Hector Hirigoyen—Miami, Florida

Audrey Jackson—Parkway School District, Chesterfield, Missouri

Jorge M. López—Puerto Rico

Susan Militello—Memphis, Tennessee

Carol Pudlin—Culver City, California

Reviewers and Consultants

Michael N. Bleicher
Professor of Mathematics
University of Wisconsin–Madison
Madison, WI

Diane J. Briars
Mathematics Specialist
Pittsburgh Public Schools
Pittsburgh, PA

Donald Chambers
Director of Dissemination
University of Wisconsin–Madison
Madison, WI

Don W. Collins
Assistant Professor of Mathematics Education
Western Kentucky University
Bowling Green, KY

Joan Elder
Mathematics Consultant
Los Angeles Unified School District
Los Angeles, CA

Elizabeth Fennema
Professor of Curriculum and Instruction
University of Wisconsin-Madison
Madison, WI

Nancy N. Gates
University of Memphis
Memphis, TN

Jane Donnelly Gawronski
Superintendent
Escondido Union High School
Escondido, CA

M. Elizabeth Graue
Assistant Professor of Curriculum and Instruction
University of Wisconsin–Madison
Madison, WI

Jodean E. Grunow
Consultant
Wisconsin Department of Public Instruction
Madison, WI

John G. Harvey
Professor of Mathematics and Curriculum & Instruction
University of Wisconsin–Madison
Madison, WI

Simon Hellerstein
Professor of Mathematics
University of Wisconsin–Madison
Madison, WI

Elaine J. Hutchinson
Senior Lecturer
University of Wisconsin–Stevens Point
Stevens Point, WI

Richard A. Johnson
Professor of Statistics
University of Wisconsin–Madison
Madison, WI

James J. Kaput
Professor of Mathematics
University of Massachusetts–Dartmouth
Dartmouth, MA

Richard Lehrer
Professor of Educational Psychology
University of Wisconsin–Madison
Madison, WI

Richard Lesh
Professor of Mathematics
University of Massachusetts–Dartmouth
Dartmouth, MA

Mary M. Lindquist
Callaway Professor of Mathematics Education
Columbus College
Columbus, GA

Baudilio (Bob) Mora
Coordinator of Mathematics & Instructional Technology
Carrollton-Farmers Branch Independent School District
Carrollton, TX

Paul Trafton
Professor of Mathematics
University of Northern Iowa
Cedar Falls, IA

Norman L. Webb
Research Scientist
University of Wisconsin–Madison
Madison, WI

Paul H. Williams
Professor of Plant Pathology
University of Wisconsin–Madison
Madison, WI

Linda Dager Wilson
Assistant Professor
University of Delaware
Newark, DE

Robert L. Wilson
Professor of Mathematics
University of Wisconsin–Madison
Madison, WI

TABLE OF CONTENTS

Dear Teacher,

Welcome! *Mathematics in Context* is designed to reflect the National Council of Teachers of Mathematics Standards for School Mathematics and to ground mathematical content in a variety of real-world contexts. Rather than relying on you to explain and demonstrate generalized definitions, rules, or algorithms, students investigate questions directly related to a particular context and construct mathematical understanding and meaning from that context.

The curriculum encompasses 10 units per grade level. This unit is designed to be the second in the number strand for grade 5/6, but it also lends itself to independent use—to informally introduce students to decimals.

In addition to the Teacher Guide and Student Books, *Mathematics in Context* offers the following components that will inform and support your teaching:

• *Teacher Resource and Implementation Guide,* which provides an overview of the complete system, including program implementation, philosophy, and rationale

• *Number Tools,* which is a series of blackline masters that serve as review sheets or practice pages involving number issues and basic skills

• *News in Numbers,* which is a set of additional activities that can be inserted between or within other units; it includes a number of measurement problems that require estimation.

• *Teacher Preparation Videos,* which present comprehensive overviews of the units to help with lesson preparation

Thank you for choosing *Mathematics in Context.* We wish you success and inspiration!

Sincerely,

The Mathematics in Context Development Team

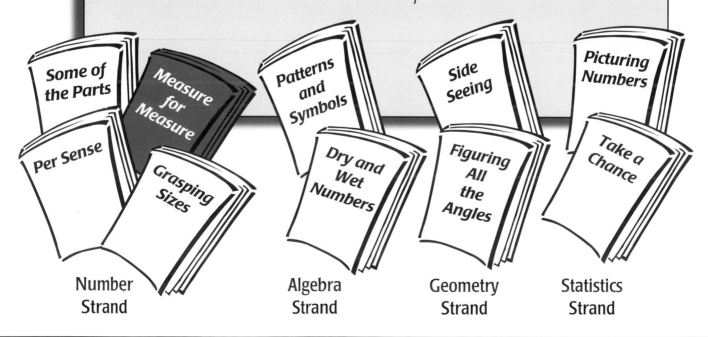

Number Strand — Some of the Parts · Per Sense · Measure for Measure · Grasping Sizes

Algebra Strand — Patterns and Symbols · Dry and Wet Numbers

Geometry Strand — Side Seeing · Figuring All the Angles

Statistics Strand — Picturing Numbers · Take a Chance

Overview

78%

How to Use This Book

This unit is one of 40 for the middle grades. Each unit can be used independently; however, the 40 units are designed to make up a complete, connected curriculum (10 units per grade level). There is a Student Book and a Teacher Guide for each unit.

Each Teacher Guide comprises elements that assist the teacher in the presentation of concepts and in understanding the general direction of the unit and the program as a whole. Becoming familiar with this structure will make using the units easier.

Each Teacher Guide consists of six basic parts:

- Overview
- Student Material and Teaching Notes
- Assessment Activities and Solutions
- Glossary
- Blackline Masters
- Try This! Solutions

Overview

Before beginning this unit, read the Overview in order to understand the purpose of the unit and to develop strategies for facilitating instruction. The Overview provides helpful information about the unit's focus, pacing, goals, and assessment, as well as explanations about how the unit fits with the rest of the *Mathematics in Context* curriculum.

Note: After reading the Overview, view the Teacher Preparation Videotape that corresponds with the strand. The video models several activities from the strand.

Student Materials and Teaching Notes

This Teacher Guide contains all of the student pages (except the Try This! activities), each of which faces a page of solutions, samples of students' work, and hints and comments about how to facilitate instruction. Note: The Try This! activities can be found in the back of this Teacher Guide.

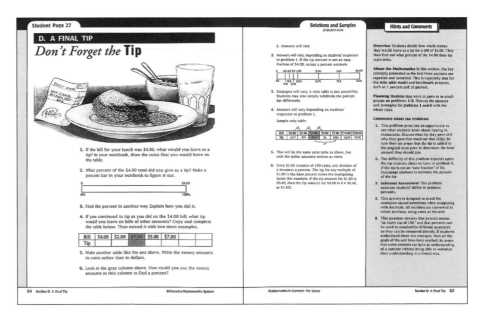

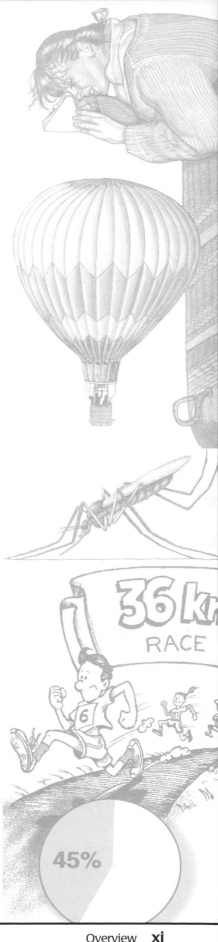

Each section within the unit begins with a two-page spread that describes the work students do, the goals of the section, new vocabulary, and materials needed, as well as providing information about the mathematics in the section and ideas for pacing, planning instruction, homework, and assessment.

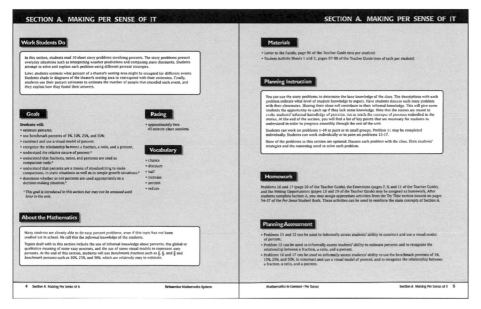

Assessment Activities and Solutions

Information about assessment can be found in several places in this Teacher Guide. General information about assessment is given in the Overview; informal assessment opportunities are identified on the teacher pages that face each student page; and the Assessment Activities section of this guide provides formal assessment opportunities.

Glossary

The Glossary defines all vocabulary words listed on the Section Opener pages. It includes mathematical terms that may be new to students, as well as words associated with the contexts introduced in the unit. (Note: The Student Book does not have a glossary. This allows students to construct their own definitions, based on their personal experiences with the unit activities.)

Blackline Masters

At the back of this Teacher Guide are blackline masters for photocopying. The blackline masters include a letter to families (to be sent home with students before beginning the unit), several student activity sheets, and assessment masters.

Try This! Solutions

Also included in the back of this Teacher Guide are the solutions to several Try This! activities—one related to each section of the unit—that can be used to reinforce the unit's main concepts. The Try This! activities are located in the back of the Student Book.

Unit Focus

In *Measure for Measure* students explore and expand their intuitive knowledge of decimals. The unit presents a variety of realistic contexts in which students begin to understand the importance of place value and create informal strategies for simple computation. Many of these informal strategies involve changing the unit of measure in a problem.

Paper strips, meter sticks, and centimeter rulers are used to help students develop their understanding of metric relationships as well as place value with decimals. Students are encouraged to build their decimal number sense and to share connections they find with each other.

Mathematical Content

- decimal place value
- rounding
- estimation
- empty number line and double number line
- relationship between fractions and decimals
- ordering decimals
- informal strategies for simple computation with decimals
- decimal number sense
- expressing units of measurement in a variety of forms
- metric units of measurement

Prior Knowledge

This unit assumes that students have worked with fractions and have seen and used the number line and the ratio table. If students need help with these topics, refer to *Number Tools.* Number knowledge from the unit *Some of the Parts* is assumed. The unit requires that students have an understanding of the following:

- using fractions to represent part-whole and division situations,
- using informal strategies to add fractions,
- representing situations involving money, using either dollars or cents.

Facility with adding and subtracting with up to three-digit numbers and facility with multiplying and dividing two-digit numbers are helpful for this unit. It is also helpful if students have had practice reading tables. Students who have already studied the unit *Patterns and Symbols* will also have had experience with repeated division by two and doubling.

Planning and Preparation

Pacing: 13–14 days

Section	Work Students Do	Pacing*	Materials
A. On Being Precise	■ work with the concept of place value using ancient Egyptian fractions ■ think about fractions, precision, and repeated division by ten as a starting point for decimals	4 days	■ Letter to the Family (one per student) ■ Student Activity Sheet 1 (one per student) ■ paper strips (two per student) ■ copies of gauges on Student Book page 2 (one per student) ■ 12-oz soda cans, optional (four or five cans per class) ■ food coloring, optional (one bottle per class) ■ wooden stick (one per class) ■ transparency, optional (one per class) ■ overhead projector, optional (one per class)
B. It Just Makes Cents	■ make connections between benchmark fractions, decimals, and division, supported by the context of money	2 days	■ Student Activity Sheets 1 and 2 (one of each per student) ■ calculators (one per student)
C. Sporting Decimals	■ interpret decimals within a sports context; the decimals refer to time, score, and distances	2 days	■ meter sticks or metric measuring tapes (one per pair of students) ■ local newspapers (about six copies per class)
D. Ordering Decimals	■ order decimals in a variety of ways ■ estimate prices, round very large numbers, and think about precision in measurement	5–6 days	■ Student Activity Sheets 3–5 (one of each per student) ■ small purchased items (such as erasers, pencils, or candy), optional (10 different items per class) ■ newspaper advertisements, optional (several ads per group) ■ transparencies of newspaper ads, optional (one or two per class) ■ overhead projector, optional (one per class) ■ atlas or almanac (one per group) ■ meter sticks, metric tape measures, or trundle wheels, optional (one per pair of students) ■ one- or two-liter container, optional (one per class)

* One day is approximately equivalent to one 45-minute class session.

Preparation

In the *Teacher Resource and Implementation Guide* is an extensive description of the philosophy underlying both the content and the pedagogy of the *Mathematics in Context* curriculum. Suggestions for preparation are also given in the Hints and Comments columns of this Teacher Guide. You may want to consider the following:

- Work through the unit before teaching it. If possible, take on the role of the student and discuss your strategies with other teachers.
- Use the overhead projector for student demonstrations, particularly with overhead transparencies of the student activity sheets and any manipulatives used in the unit.
- Invite students to use drawings and examples to illustrate and clarify their answers.
- Allow students to work at different levels of sophistication. Some students may need concrete materials, while others can work at a more abstract level.
- Provide opportunities and support for students to share their strategies, which often differ. This allows students to take part in class discussions and introduces them to alternative ways to think about the mathematics in the unit.
- In some cases, it may be necessary to read the problems to students or to pair students to facilitate their understanding of the printed materials.
- A list of the materials needed for this unit is in the chart on page xiii.
- Try to follow the recommended pacing chart on page xiii. You can easily spend more time on this unit than the number of class periods indicated. Bear in mind, however, that many of the topics introduced in this unit will be revisited and covered more thoroughly in other *Mathematics in Context* units.

Resources

For Teachers	For Students
Books and Magazines • *Mathematics Assessment: Myths, Models, Good Questions, and Practical Suggestions*, edited by Jean Kerr Stenmark (Reston, Virginia: The National Council of Teachers of Mathematics, Inc., 1991) • *Ancient Egyptian Materials and Industries*, by A. Lucas and J.R. Harris (London:1989)	**Tools** Students are expected to have calculators available. However, the intention of this unit is not to teach students "smart calculator tricks" to deal with decimals. This unit focuses on understanding of decimals and how to calculate with them.
Videos *Number Strand Teacher Preparation Video*	**Videos** *MathSense Video How Decimals Work* (available from Encyclopædia Britannica)

Assessment

Planning Assessment

In keeping with the NCTM Assessment Standards, valid assessment should be based on evidence drawn from several sources. (See the full discussion of assessment philosophies in the *Teacher Resource and Implementation Guide*.) An assessment plan for this unit may draw from the following sources:

- Observations—look, listen, and record observable behavior.

- Interactive Responses—in a teacher-facilitated situation, note how students respond, clarify, revise, and extend their thinking.

- Products—look for the quality of thought evident in student projects, test answers, worksheet solutions, or writings.

These categories are not meant to be mutually exclusive. In fact, observation is a key part of assessing interactive responses and also key to understanding the end results of projects and writings.

Ongoing Assessment Opportunities

- **Problems within Sections**
  To evaluate ongoing progress, *Mathematics in Context* identifies informal assessment opportunities and the goals that these particular problems assess throughout the Teacher Guide. There are also indications as to what you might expect from your students.

- **Section Summary Questions**
  The summary questions at the end of each section are vehicles for informal assessment (see Teacher Guide pages 28, 42, 56, and 82).

End-of-Unit Assessment Opportunities

In the back of this Teacher Guide, there are three assessment activities, that, when combined, form a one–class period end-of-unit assessment. For a more detailed description of the assessment activities, see the Assessment Overview (Teacher Guide pages 84 and 85).

You may also wish to design your own culminating project or let students create one that will tell you what they consider is important in the unit. For more assessment ideas, refer to the chart on pages xvi and xvii.

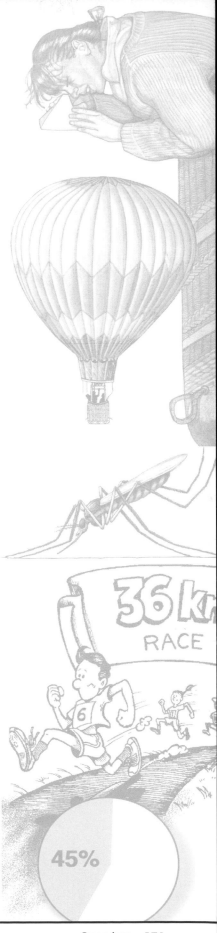

78%

Goals and Assessment

In the *Mathematics in Context* curriculum, unit goals, categorized according to cognitive procedures, relate to the strand goals and the NCTM Curriculum and Evaluation Standards. Additional information about these goals is found in the *Teacher Resource and Implementation Guide.* The *Mathematics in Context* curriculum is designed to help students develop their abilities so that they can perform with understanding in each of the categories listed below. It is important to note that the attainment of goals in one category is not a prerequisite to attaining those in another category. In fact, students should progress simultaneously toward several goals in different categories.

	Goal	Ongoing Assessment Opportunities	End-of-Unit Assessment Opportunities
Conceptual and Procedural Knowledge	**1.** understand the relationship between benchmark fractions and their decimal representations	**Section B** p. 36, #7 p. 38, #14	Penny Tube, p. 100, #1–4
	2. use decimals in a context, such as money or measurement	**Section B** p. 42, #19 **Section C** p. 46, #2 p. 56, #20	Penny Tube, p. 100, #1 and 2 Metric Units, p. 101, #3 The Bakery, p. 102, #1
	3. estimate and compute with decimals	**Section A** p. 26, #19 **Section C** p. 52, #16 **Section D** p. 67, Extension	Metric Units, p. 101, #3 The Bakery, p. 102, #1 and 2

	Goal	Ongoing Assessment Opportunities		End-of-Unit Assessment Opportunities
Reasoning, Communicating, Thinking, and Making Connections	**4.** understand place value and its use in ordering decimals	**Section A** **Section C** **Section D**	p. 26, #18 p. 46, #2 p. 52, #15,#16 p. 56, #20 p. 62, #2, #3 p. 80, #32	The Bakery, p. 102, #1
	5. understand the metric system and its relationship to decimals	**Section C** **Section D**	p. 56, #20 p. 78, #29 p. 80, #32	Metric Units, p. 101, #1–3
	6. understand decimals as they relate to refinement in the measurement process	**Section A** **Section D**	p. 28, #20, #21 p. 74, #22, #23 p. 82, #34	Metric Units, p. 101, #3

	Goal	Ongoing Assessment Opportunities		End-of-Unit Assessment Opportunities
Modeling, Nonroutine Problem-Solving, Critically Analyzing, and Generalizing	**7.** use equivalent representations of fractions, decimals, and division notation	**Section A** **Section B**	p. 10, #4 p. 36, #7 p. 38, #14 p. 40, #16 p. 42, #19	Penny Tube, p. 100, #1–4
	8. represent and use decimals in a variety of equivalent forms to solve problems in real-world and mathematical situations	**Section C**	p. 56, #20	Penny Tube, p. 100, #2
	9. choose an appropriate visual model or strategy to represent and solve problems involving decimals	**Section C** **Section D**	p. 52, #15, #16 p. 78, #29	Penny Tube, p. 100, #1 Metric Units, p. 101, #3 The Bakery, p. 102, #1 and 2

More about Assessment

Scoring and Analyzing Assessment Responses

Students may respond to assessment questions with various levels of mathematical sophistication and elaboration. Each student's response should be considered for the mathematics that it shows, and not judged on whether or not it includes an expected response. Responses to some of the assessment questions may be viewed as either correct or incorrect, but many answers will need flexible judgment by the teacher. Descriptive judgments related to specific goals and partial credit often provide more helpful feedback than percentage scores.

Openly communicate your expectations to all students, and report achievement and progress for each student relative to those expectations. When scoring students' responses try to think about how they are progressing toward the goals of the unit and the strand.

Student Portfolios

Generally, a portfolio is a collection of student-selected pieces that is representative of a student's work. A portfolio may include evaluative comments by you or by the student. See the *Teacher Resource and Implementation Guide* for more ideas on portfolio focus and use.

A comprehensive discussion about the contents, management, and evaluation of portfolios can be found in *Mathematics Assessment: Myths, Models, Good Questions, and Practical Suggestions,* pp. 35–48.

Student Self-Evaluation

Self-evaluation encourages students to reflect on their progress in learning mathematical concepts, their developing abilities to use mathematics, and their dispositions toward mathematics. The following examples illustrate ways to incorporate student self-evaluations as one component of your assessment plan.

- Ask students to comment, in writing, on each piece they have chosen for their portfolios and on the progress they see in the pieces overall.
- Give a writing assignment entitled "What I Know Now about [a math concept] and What I Think about It." This will give you information about each student's disposition toward mathematics as well as his or her knowledge.
- Interview individuals or small groups to elicit what they have learned, what they think is important, and why.

Suggestions for self-inventories can be found in *Mathematics Assessment: Myths, Models, Good Questions, and Practical Suggestions,* pp. 55–58.

Summary Discussion

Discuss specific lessons and activities in the unit—what the student learned from them and what the activities have in common. This can be done in whole-class discussions, small groups, or in personal interviews.

Connections across the *Mathematics in Context* Curriculum

Measure for Measure is the second unit in the number strand. The map below shows the complete *Mathematics in Context* curriculum for grade 5/6. It indicates where the unit fits in the number strand and where it fits in the overall picture.

A detailed description of the units, the strands, and the connections in the *Mathematics in Context* curriculum can be found in the *Teacher Resource and Implementation Guide.*

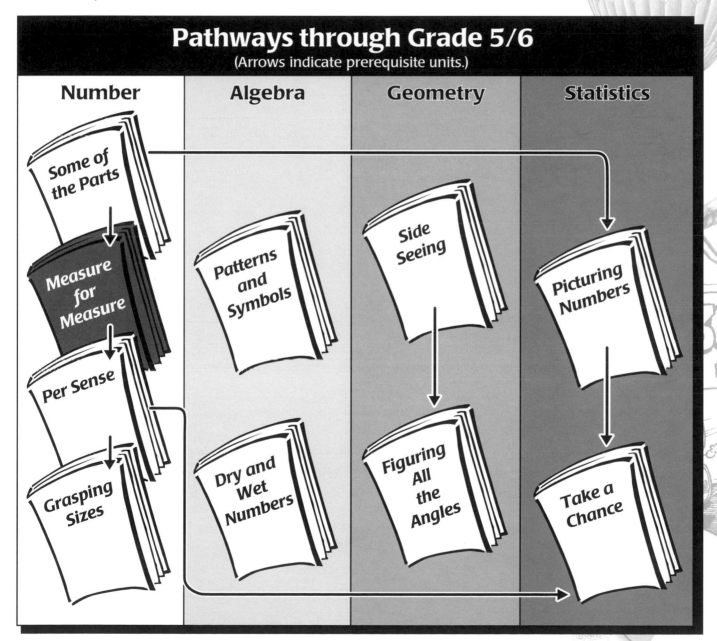

Pathways through Grade 5/6
(Arrows indicate prerequisite units.)

Number	Algebra	Geometry	Statistics

Some of the Parts

Measure for Measure

Per Sense

Grasping Sizes

Patterns and Symbols

Dry and Wet Numbers

Side Seeing

Figuring All the Angles

Picturing Numbers

Take a Chance

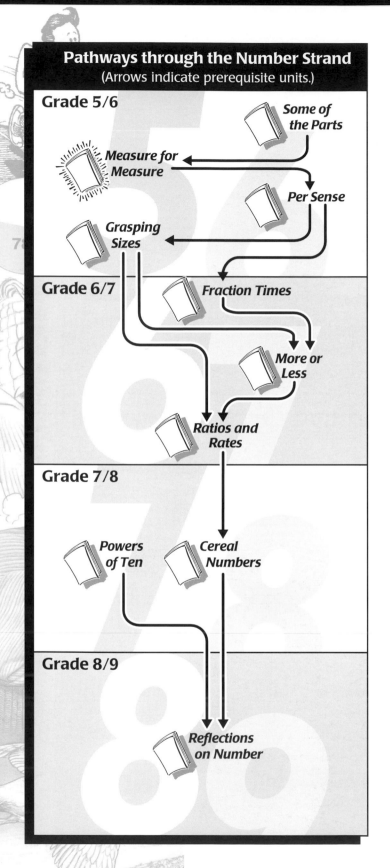

Pathways through the Number Strand
(Arrows indicate prerequisite units.)

Grade 5/6

Some of the Parts

Measure for Measure

Per Sense

Grasping Sizes

Grade 6/7

Fraction Times

More or Less

Ratios and Rates

Grade 7/8

Powers of Ten

Cereal Numbers

Grade 8/9

Reflections on Number

Connections within the Number Strand

On the left is a map of the number strand; this unit, *Measure for Measure*, is highlighted.

Measure for Measure is the second unit in the number strand and is preceded by *Some of the Parts*. *Measure for Measure* builds on the fraction concepts that are introduced in *Some of the Parts*, as well as the notions of measurement and precision as a starting point for decimals. *Some of the Parts* provides a foundation for using the number line for estimation. Extra practice with the number line is available in *Number Tools*.

Decimals are revisited in *Fraction Times*, *More or Less*, and *Ratios and Rates*. More opportunities to use connections among fractions, decimals, and percents are found in the unit *Cereal Numbers*.

The Number Strand

Grade 5/6

Some of the Parts
Using fractions to describe the relative magnitude of quantities; ordering fractions; and understanding performing addition, subtraction, and multiplication, and division operations with fractions.

Measure for Measure
Representing and using decimals in a variety of equivalent forms, investigating relationships among fractions and decimals, extending decimal number sense, and adding and subtracting decimals.

Per Sense
Understanding percents as representing part-whole relationships; understanding the relationship between fractions, percents, and ratios; and developing strategies for estimating and calculating percents.

Grasping Sizes
Developing a conceptual sense of ratio, estimating and calculating the effects of proportional enlargements or reductions, using scale lines, organizing data into ratio tables and calculating ratios, and writing fractions as alternative expressions for equivalence situations.

Grade 6/7

Fraction Times
Comparing, adding, subtracting, and multiplying fractions and understanding the relationship among fractions, percents, decimals, and ratios.

More or Less
Connecting fractions, decimals, and percents; exploring percents as operators; and discovering the effects of decimal multiplication.

Ratios and Rates
Relating ratios to fractions, decimals, and percents; dividing with decimals; differentiating between part-part and part-whole ratios; and understanding the notions of rate, scale factor, and ratio as linear functions.

Grade 7/8

Cereal Numbers
Measuring volume and surface area in metric units; noting how changes in volume affect changes in the surface area of rectangular prisms; making comparisons with ratios, fractions, decimals, and percents; using a visual model to multiply with fractions; and using a ratio strategy to divide with fractions.

Powers of Ten
Investigating simple laws for calculating with powers of 10, and investigating very large and very small numbers.

Grade 8/9

Reflections on Number
Exploring primes, prime factorization, and divisibility rules; analyzing algorithms for multiplication and division; and discovering and relating whole numbers, integers, and rational and irrational numbers by looking at the results of basic operations with their inverses.

Connections with Other *Mathematics in Context* Units

The measurement concepts introduced in *Some of the Parts* are covered in greater depth in *Measure for Measure* and further extended in *Made to Measure*. The notions of repeated halving and doubling are also explored in *Patterns and Symbols, Ups and Downs*, and *Growth*. Metric measurement is further investigated in other *Mathematics in Context* units, such as *Fraction Times, Ratios and Rates*, and *More or Less*. Students work with fractions, decimals, and division concepts in all the number units as well as in the units *Picturing Numbers, Dealing with Data*, and *Tracking Graphs*.

The following mathematical topics that are included in the unit *Measure for Measure* are introduced or further developed in other *Mathematics in Context* units:

Prerequisite Topics

Topic	Unit	Grade
fractions, measurement, notion of precision	*Some of the Parts*	5/6
number line, ratio table	*Number Tools*	5/6
double number line	*Some of the Parts*	5/6
fraction bar	*Some of the Parts*	5/6

Topics Revisited in Other Units

Topic	Unit	Grade
repeated halving/doubling	*Some of the Parts*	5/6
	Patterns and Symbols**	5/6
	Ups and Downs**	7/8
	Growth**	8/9
metric measurement	*Fraction Times*	6/7
	Ratios and Rates	6/7
	More or Less	6/7
	Made to Measure***	6/7
fractions/decimals/division	all number units	
	Picturing Numbers*	5/6
	Dealing with Data*	6/7
	Tracking Graphs**	6/7

* These units in the statistics strand also help students make connections to ideas about numbers.
** These units in the algebra strand also help students make connections to ideas about numbers.
*** These units in the geometry strand also help students make connections to ideas about numbers.

Student Materials and Teaching Notes

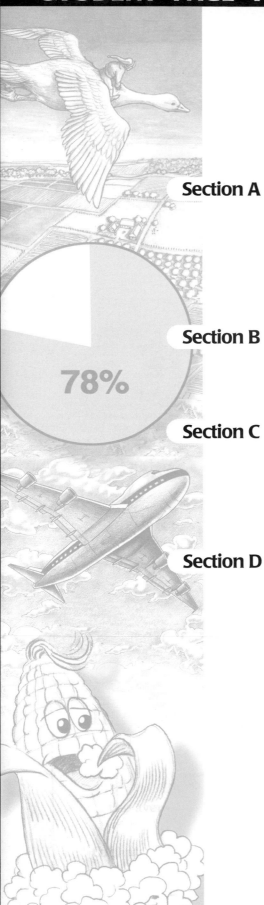

78%

Student Book
Table of Contents

Dear Student,

Welcome to *Measure for Measure*.

Throughout this unit, you will study concepts related to decimals. You will study the relationship between fractions and decimals, decimal place value, rounding, estimating, and ordering decimals. You will be introduced to informal strategies for simple computations, decimal number sense, and metric units of measure.

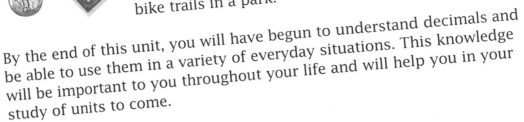

Having worked with money in everyday situations, you already know a lot about decimals. This unit will encourage you to explore and add to what you already know.

You will be investigating the ancient Egyptian number systems, calculating combinations of coins in order to purchase items, ranking singers in an amateur talent show, estimating the number of pennies in a collection tube, ordering and rounding population numbers, and measuring distances and speeds for bike trails in a park.

By the end of this unit, you will have begun to understand decimals and be able to use them in a variety of everyday situations. This knowledge will be important to you throughout your life and will help you in your study of units to come.

Sincerely,

The Mathematics in Context Development Team

Work Students Do

As an introduction to precision in measurement, students measure common objects using paper strips of arbitrary length. They also read gauges to estimate how many liters are in water tanks and use a fraction to describe the part of each tank that is full. Students translate ancient Egyptian fractions in a context that combines fact and fiction, and explore two different number systems: one based on repeated halving and the other based on repeated division by ten. Students' investigations of fractions and precision in measurement serve as springboards for understanding decimals.

Goals

Students will:

• understand place value and its use in ordering decimals;

• estimate and compute with decimals;

• use equivalent representations of fractions, decimals, and division notation;

• understand decimals as they relate to refinement in the measurement process.

Pacing

• approximately four 45-minute class sessions

Vocabulary

• benchmark fraction

• fraction bar

• liter

• precision in measurement

About the Mathematics

Two different number systems are contrasted in this section. The first system, used by the ancient Egyptians, is based on repeated halving. It does not use place value notation. The second system, used by the fictitious Cleopatra and Daughters Company, is based on repeated division by ten. It is similar to our decimal system; however, it does not use the concept of place-value. This number system introduces the concept of *precision in measurement*. By subdividing the measuring unit (one turn of a wheel) into 10 parts and further subdividing those 10 parts, a more precise measurement is possible. An exploration of fractions leads to an understanding of decimal-fraction equivalencies.

The *fraction bar* is used as a visual model with which students can make estimations. The fraction bar is introduced in the grade 5/6 unit *Some of the Parts* and is used extensively in the grade 5/6 unit *Per Sense* to develop students' understanding of percents and their ability to estimate.

Materials

- Letter to the Family, page 94 of the Teacher Guide (one per student)
- Student Activity Sheet 1, page 95 of the Teacher Guide (one per student)
- paper strips, pages 7, 11, 13, and 17 of the Teacher Guide (four per student)
- copies of gauges on Student Book page 2, page 9 of the Teacher Guide, optional (one per student)
- 12-oz soda cans, page 15 of the Teacher Guide, optional (four or five 12 oz. cans per class)
- food coloring, page 15 of the Teacher Guide, optional (one bottle per class)
- wooden stick, page 15 of the Teacher Guide, optional (one per class)
- transparency, pages 23 and 25 of the Teacher Guide, optional (one per class)
- overhead projector, pages 23 and 25 of the Teacher Guide, optional (one per class)

Planning Instruction

The first activity in this section, involving measuring strips, introduces the concept of precision in measurement and sets the stage for using Egyptian fractions. It is recommended that you provide students with paper strips for this activity. If students make their own measuring strips, the measurement units will vary from one paper strip to another. In this case, students may not grasp the fixed nature of a measurement unit.

Students may work on problems 1–8 and 13 in pairs or in small groups. They may work individually or in pairs on the remaining problems. Be sure to discuss students' solutions and strategies for problems 1, 4, 6, 7d, 8d and e, 15, and 16.

There are no optional problems in this section.

Homework

Problems 5 (page 12 of the Teacher Guide) and 10–12 (page 20 of the Teacher Guide) can be assigned as homework. The Extension (page 13 of the Teacher Guide), the Bringing Math Home activity (page 7 of the Teacher Guide), and the Community Connection (page 15 of the Teacher Guide) can also be assigned as homework. After students complete Section A, you may assign appropriate activities from the Try This! section, located on pages 37–40 of the *Measure for Measure* Student Book. The Try This! activities reinforce the key math concepts introduced in this section.

Planning Assessment

- Problem 4 can be used to informally assess students' ability to use equivalent representations of fractions, decimals, and division notation.
- Problem 18 can be used to informally assesses students' understanding of place value and its use in ordering decimals.
- Problem 19 can be used to informally assess students' ability to estimate and compute with decimals.
- Problems 20 and 21 can be used to informally assess students' understanding of decimals as they relate to refinement in the measurement process.

A. ON BEING PRECISE

Marks and Measures

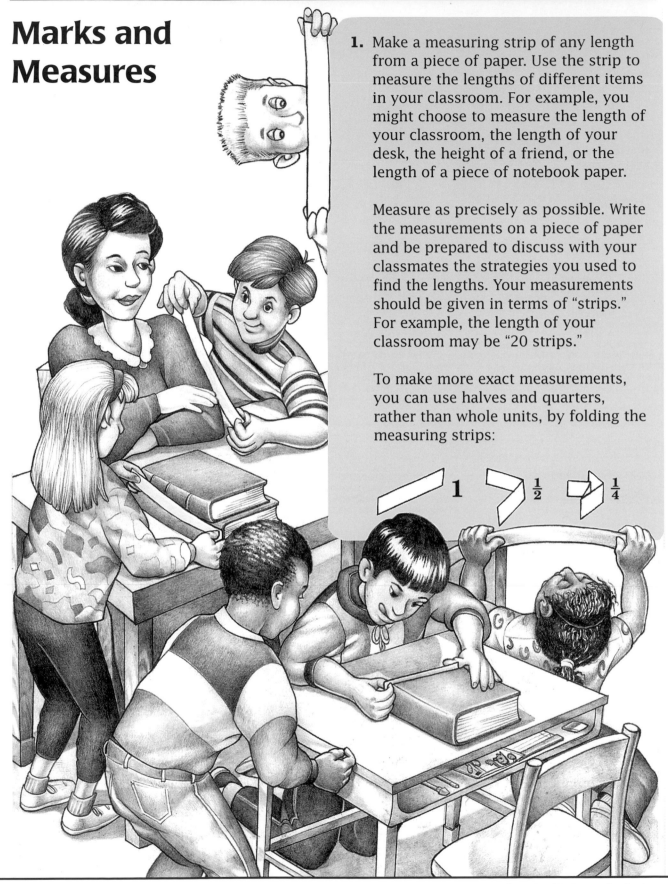

1. Make a measuring strip of any length from a piece of paper. Use the strip to measure the lengths of different items in your classroom. For example, you might choose to measure the length of your classroom, the length of your desk, the height of a friend, or the length of a piece of notebook paper.

   Measure as precisely as possible. Write the measurements on a piece of paper and be prepared to discuss with your classmates the strategies you used to find the lengths. Your measurements should be given in terms of "strips." For example, the length of your classroom may be "20 strips."

   To make more exact measurements, you can use halves and quarters, rather than whole units, by folding the measuring strips:

   1 $\frac{1}{2}$ $\frac{1}{4}$

Solutions and Samples
of student work

1. Answers will vary. Some students may give their answers to the nearest half or fourth of a strip. Others may express their answers to the nearest whole strip.

Hints and Comments

Materials paper strips (one per student)

Overview Students use paper strips to measure various classroom objects. To measure more precisely, they may use halves and quarters of the strips.

About the Mathematics This activity is directly linked to the preceding grade 5/6 unit *Some of the Parts*, in which students work with fraction strips and use fractions to describe part-whole relationships.

The activity also sets the stage for the introduction of Egyptian fractions on page 3 of the Student Book.

Planning If you decide to let students use paper strips of different lengths, you may use different colors to signify the varying lengths. This will facilitate later discussions about using different measuring units and the need for standardization.

Before students begin problem **1,** discuss how to fold and mark the strips to show halves and fourths. Students may work in pairs or in small groups on problem **1.** Discuss the problem with the whole class.

Comments about the Problems

1. Students can learn a variety of ways to express measurements from their classmates' answers. For example, students may express their answer as two and a half strips, $2 + \frac{1}{2}$ strips, 2 strips and $\frac{1}{2}$ strip, or $2\frac{1}{2}$ strips.

   Invite students to share how they determined the lengths of various objects. Some may have folded and divided their strips into halves or fourths, making a type of ruler with equal divisions. Ask students how they could make their measurements even more precise. One possible answer is by folding the paper into eighths.

Bringing Math Home Ask each student to estimate the length and width of his or her kitchen using a measuring strip. Have students find the actual dimensions when they get home. The next day, discuss with them how close their estimates were to the actual dimensions.

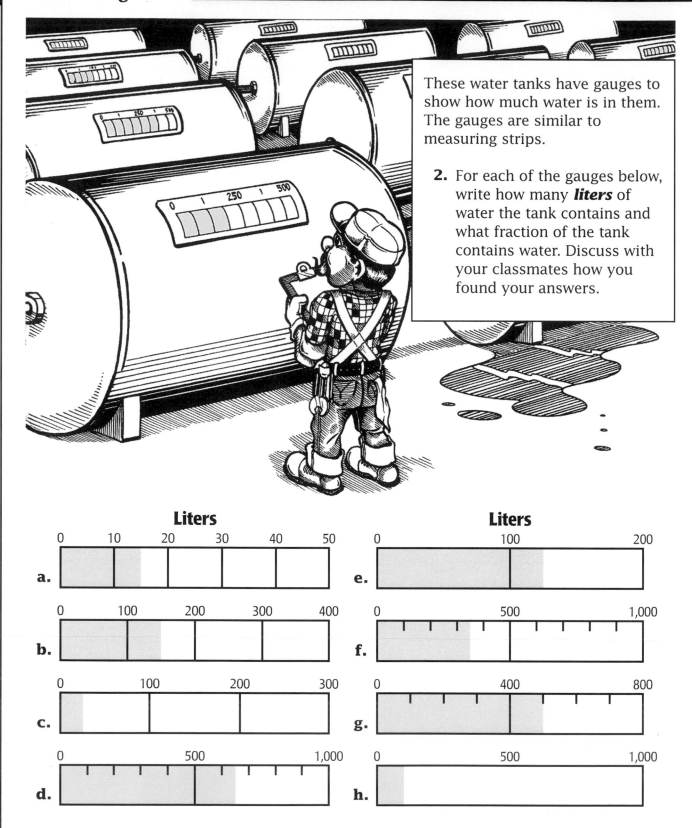

These water tanks have gauges to show how much water is in them. The gauges are similar to measuring strips.

2. For each of the gauges below, write how many *liters* of water the tank contains and what fraction of the tank contains water. Discuss with your classmates how you found your answers.

Liters

a.
0   10   20   30   40   50

b.
0   100   200   300   400

c.
0   100   200   300

d.
0   500   1,000

Liters

e.
0   100   200

f.
0   500   1,000

g.
0   400   800

h.
0   500   1,000

A measuring strip is like a gauge. For example, if a gauge measures a total of 50 liters and you think of it as one whole strip, then the 25-liter mark is like $\frac{1}{2}$ of a strip.

2. a. about 15 liters, or $\frac{3}{10}$ of the tank

    b. about 150 liters, or $\frac{3}{8}$ of the tank

    c. about 25 liters, or $\frac{1}{12}$ of the tank

    d. about 650 liters, or $\frac{13}{20}$ of the tank

    e. about 125 liters, or $\frac{5}{8}$ of the tank

    f. about 350 liters, or $\frac{7}{20}$ of the tank

    g. about 500 liters, or $\frac{5}{8}$ of the tank

    h. about 100 liters, or $\frac{1}{10}$ of the tank

Materials copies of gauges on Student Book page 2, optional (one per student)

Overview Students read gauges on water tanks to estimate how many liters of water are in each tank. They also use a fraction to describe the part of each tank that is full.

About the Mathematics Both the water gauges and the paper strips are similar to the *fraction bar* model. Students are first introduced to the fraction bar model in the grade 5/6 unit *Some of the Parts*. On this page, they estimate what part of each tank is full using fraction bars and *benchmark fractions*, such as $\frac{1}{2}$, $\frac{1}{4}$, and $\frac{3}{4}$.

They may also implicitly use fractions as operators to determine how many liters of water are in each tank. For example, in problem **2a,** students may first read the gauge to determine that the tank is $\frac{3}{10}$ full and then multiply $\frac{3}{10} \times 50$ to find that the tank contains 15 liters.

Planning You may want to discuss what a metric liter is and what a water gauge does before beginning this activity. Students should be able to use benchmark fractions to describe part-whole relationships. If students are not familiar with these common fractions, you may want to have them create several gauges (or paper strips) with measuring lines indicating halves, thirds, fourths, and other fractional parts. Students should not use calculators to estimate. They may work in pairs or in small groups on this problem.

Comments about the Problems

    2. If students are having difficulty estimating fractions, you may want to photocopy the water gauges (on page 8 of the Teacher Guide) so that students can then cut them out and fold them (or make division marks) to estimate the fraction represented by the shaded part of each gauge. Encourage students to share their estimation strategies.

Egyptian Fractions

The only fractions that the ancient Egyptians used had numerators of 1. Other fractions were written as a combination of these fractions. For example, $\frac{3}{4}$ could be written as:

$$\frac{1}{2} + \frac{1}{4} \quad or \quad \frac{1}{4} + \frac{1}{4} + \frac{1}{4}$$

The oldest system used by the Egyptians was based on halving (dividing by two). Each fraction had its own symbol.

Here are some of the fraction symbols.

$\frac{1}{2}$ ◁ $\frac{1}{4}$ ◯ $\frac{1}{8}$ ⌒

$\frac{1}{16}$ ▷— $\frac{1}{32}$ ⌇◉ $\frac{1}{64}$ ◸

3. Look at the pattern of fractions. What would be the next fraction? Make up a symbol for it.

4. Find the following sums.

a. ⌒ + ⌒

b. ▷ + ▷ + ⌒

c. ◁ + ◯ + ⌒ + ⌒

HORUS

Above is a drawing of Horus, a god in ancient Egyptian religion. Horus took the form of a falcon. One of Horus's eyes was the sun. The other eye, the one in the picture, was the moon. According to mythology, the god of darkness ripped Horus's moon eye into several pieces, and that explained why the moon changes shape.

3. Students may create a variety of symbols. However, the symbols should represent $\frac{1}{2}$ of $\frac{1}{64}$, or $\frac{1}{128}$.

4. **a.** $\overset{\frown}{} + \overset{\frown}{}$

   $= \frac{1}{8} + \frac{1}{8} = \frac{2}{8}$, or $\frac{1}{4}$

   b. $\triangleright + \triangleright + \overset{\frown}{}$

   $= \frac{1}{16} + \frac{1}{16} + \frac{1}{8} = \frac{4}{16}$, or $\frac{1}{4}$

   or

   $\frac{1}{16} + \frac{1}{16} + \frac{1}{8} = \frac{1}{8} + \frac{1}{8} = \frac{2}{8}$, or $\frac{1}{4}$

   or

   $\frac{1}{16} + \frac{1}{16} + \frac{1}{16} + \frac{1}{16} = \frac{4}{16}$, or $\frac{2}{8}$, or $\frac{1}{4}$

   c. $\triangleleft + \bigcirc + \overset{\frown}{} + \overset{\frown}{}$

   $= \frac{1}{2} + \frac{1}{4} + \frac{1}{8} + \frac{1}{8} = \frac{8}{8}$, or 1

   or

   $\frac{1}{2} + \frac{1}{4} + \frac{1}{8} + \frac{1}{8} = \frac{1}{2} + \frac{1}{4} + \frac{1}{4} = \frac{1}{2} + \frac{1}{2} = 1$

   or

   $\frac{4}{8} + \frac{2}{8} + \frac{1}{8} + \frac{1}{8} = \frac{8}{8}$, or 1

Materials paper strips (one per student)

Overview Students are introduced to the symbols that the ancient Egyptians used to express fractions. They then identify and find the sums of various fraction symbols.

About the Mathematics The ancient Egyptian number system introduced on this page is based on repeated halving; it does not use place-value notation. The number system introduced on page 9 of the Student Book is based on repeated division by ten. This second system, although it does not use place-value notation, is similar to our decimal number system.

If students have already completed the grade 5/6 unit *Patterns and Symbols*, they will be familiar with the concept of repeated halving. If not, the activities in this section will give students a better understanding of this concept.

Planning Students can work on problems **3** and **4** in pairs or in small groups. Discuss problem **4** with students.

Comments about the Problems

3. You can refer to the first problem in this section to help students make connections between the concrete paper strips and the fraction symbols used here. Discuss with students how they determined their answers. It is important to mention that halving $\frac{1}{64}$ results in $\frac{1}{128}$.

4. **Informal Assessment** This problem assesses students' ability to use equivalent representations of fractions, decimals, and division notation.

   If students only "translate" these fraction sums, encourage them to write a shorter answer. Students may use their knowledge of equivalent fractions to express their answers in simplest form. For example, in solving problem **4a,** students may compute $\frac{1}{8} + \frac{1}{8} = \frac{2}{8} = \frac{1}{4}$. They may also use the fraction pattern shown in the picture to reason that $\frac{1}{8}$ is half of $\frac{1}{4}$, so $\frac{1}{8} + \frac{1}{8}$ equals $\frac{1}{4}$.

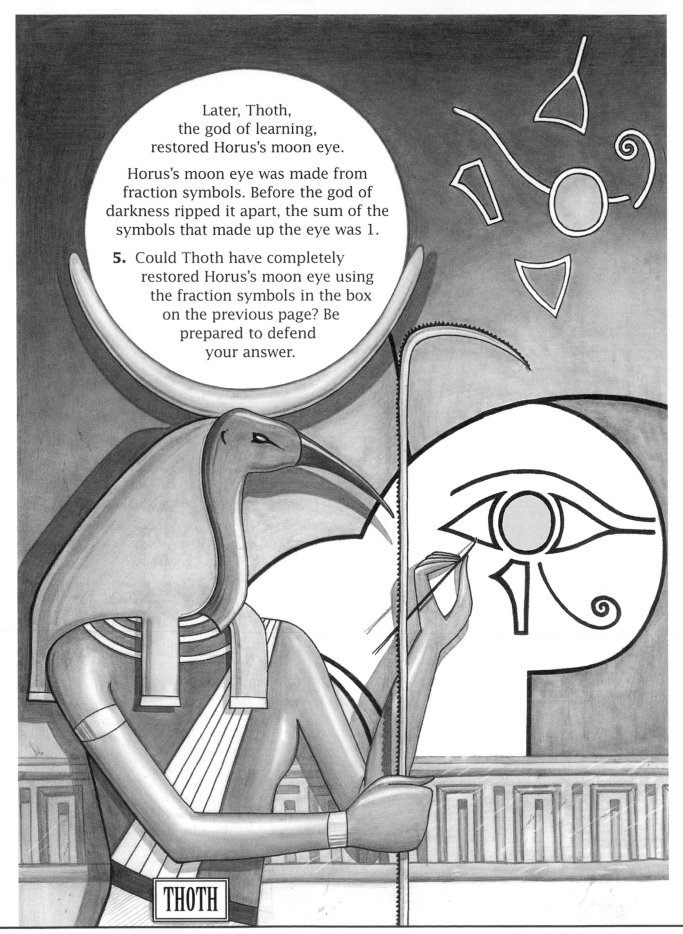

Later, Thoth, the god of learning, restored Horus's moon eye.

Horus's moon eye was made from fraction symbols. Before the god of darkness ripped it apart, the sum of the symbols that made up the eye was 1.

5. Could Thoth have completely restored Horus's moon eye using the fraction symbols in the box on the previous page? Be prepared to defend your answer.

THOTH

5. No. The fractions from the pictured eye add up to $\frac{63}{64}$, rather than 1.

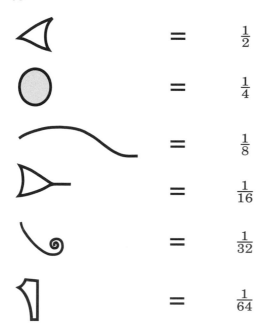

(triangle)	=	$\frac{1}{2}$
(oval)	=	$\frac{1}{4}$
(curve)	=	$\frac{1}{8}$
(eye with triangle)	=	$\frac{1}{16}$
(spiral)	=	$\frac{1}{32}$
(leaf shape)	=	$\frac{1}{64}$

Some students may use a fraction bar to illustrate the same idea:

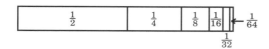

So, the fraction bar will never be filled in to make one whole.

Materials paper strips (one per student)

Overview Students translate and add the Egyptian fraction symbols shown on page 3 of the Student Book to see whether their sum is equal to one. According to the Egyptian legend, if the sum of the fraction symbols is equal to one, Thoth can use these symbols to completely restore Horus's moon eye.

Planning Students can work on problem **5** in pairs or in small groups. You may assign this problem as homework. Discuss students' solutions and strategies for this problem.

Comments about the Problems

5. Homework This problem may be assigned as homework. Encourage students to make a strip marked with repeated halvings and to draw the Egyptian fraction symbols on the strip. While working on this problem, students may discover that the sum of the fraction series $\frac{1}{2} + \frac{1}{4} + \frac{1}{8} + \frac{1}{16}$ ... will never equal 1.

Extension Encourage students to solve the following math puzzle, which uses the same underlying math principle as problem **5:**

A frog is one meter from a wall. With each jump, the frog hops half of the remaining distance to the wall. Its first jump is $\frac{1}{2}$ meter, its second jump is $\frac{1}{4}$ meter, its third jump is $\frac{1}{8}$ meter, and so on. Will the frog ever reach the wall? [No. Using the concept of repeated halving, dividing any fractional unit by two will never result in an answer of zero. Therefore, in theory, the frog will never reach the wall.]

Castor Oil

Ancient Egyptians used castor oil on their bodies, in their lamps, and as medicine. Production of this oil required a lot of measuring.

The following story is about a make-believe Egyptian company.

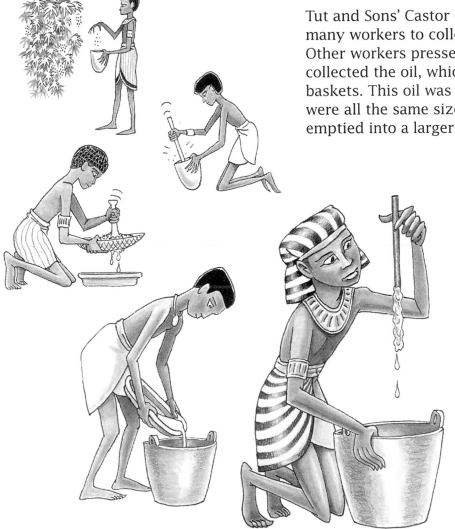

Tut and Sons' Castor Oil Company employed many workers to collect beans and grind them. Other workers pressed the ground beans and collected the oil, which dripped through the baskets. This oil was collected in pans that were all the same size. The pans were then emptied into a larger bucket.

To keep track of the amount of oil in the bucket, the workers made measuring rods.

When a measuring rod was dipped into a bucket, oil remained on the rod. Because the measuring rods were marked to indicate the amount of oil in one full pan, the oil in the buckets could easily be measured in terms of pans.

Materials 12 oz. soda cans, optional (four or five cans per class); food coloring, optional (one bottle per class); wooden stick, optional (one per class)

Overview Students read about how a fictional Egyptian company made castor oil and how the workers used measuring rods to record the amounts of oil in each bucket. There are no problems to solve on this page.

Planning You may want to read the text on this page aloud with students and discuss the use of a dipstick to measure oil levels. You may also demonstrate how a dipstick works using the following activity:

Gather four or five empty 12-ounce cans and fill them with different levels of water. Color the water with food coloring. Use a wooden stick as a dipstick to measure and compare the amounts of water in each can.

Did You Know? Castor oil was indeed collected and extracted by the ancient Egyptians, as described on the facing page. For more information, read *Ancient Egyptian Materials and Industries,* by A. Lucas and J. R. Harris (London: 1989). The companies, measuring rods, and sacred ritual described in the story, however, are fictional.

Community Connection Suggest that students interview a mechanic in their community to investigate how a dipstick is used to check the oil level in a car's engine. Students might ask some of the following questions: *How much oil is in a full tank? What amounts do the different lines on the dipstick correspond to? Do the oil levels differ from one car model to another?* [Answers will vary. Typical answers may include the following: five quarts; the top line shows full and the next line indicates one quart below full; oil levels can vary from car to car.] Students can report their findings to the class.

6. How much oil is shown on measuring rods *a* through *e* (shown below)? Use a paper measuring strip to find the amounts.

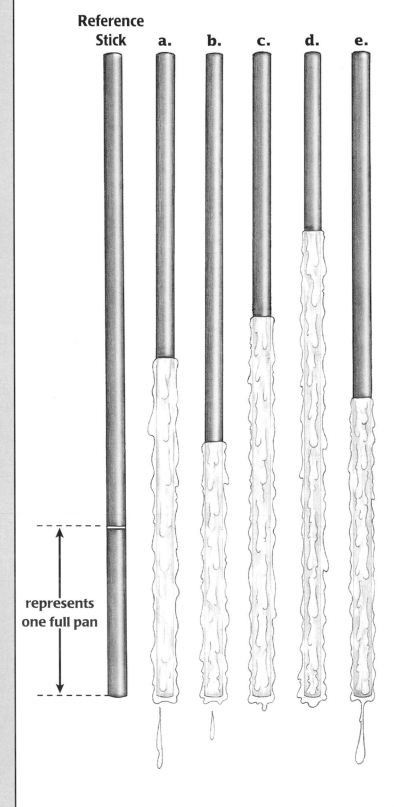

Reference
Stick   a.   b.   c.   d.   e.

represents
one full pan

The castor oil workers measured the amount of oil in units of $1, \frac{1}{2}, \frac{1}{4}, \frac{1}{8}$, and $\frac{1}{16}$ of a pan. To keep track of the measurements, they used combinations of the symbols mentioned earlier.

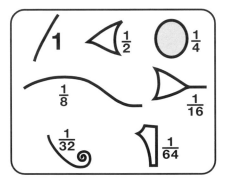

Thus, 1 and $\frac{1}{4}$ pans would be written as:

Ancient Egyptians wrote and read from right to left, instead of from left to right as we do. In order to make it easier to compare our number system to that of the Egyptians, all Egyptian numbers in this unit will be written from left to right.

For example, we will write $1\frac{1}{4}$ pans as:

7. Use the symbols for Egyptian fractions to write the amounts of castor oil shown on measuring rods *a* through *e*.

6. a. 2 pans

   b. $1\frac{1}{2}$ pans

   c. $2\frac{1}{4}$ pans

   d. $2\frac{3}{4}$ pans

   e. $1\frac{3}{4}$ pans

7. Answers may vary. Sample answers:

   a. //

   b. /◁   or / ○○

   c. //○   or //～

   d. //◁○ or //○○○

   e. /◁○   or /○○○

Material paper strips (one per student)

Overview Students look at drawings of measuring rods that represent the number of pans of caster oil in five different buckets. Students use the height of one "pan" shown in the drawing and paper strips to describe the amounts using both common fractions and Egyptian symbols.

Planning Before students begin this problem, make sure they realize that the pans are all the same size. Students can work in pairs or in small groups on problems **6** and **7.** Be sure to discuss at least problems **6** and **7d,** and have students share their problem-solving strategies.

Comments about the Problems

   6. Students should estimate rather than measure the exact amounts.

7. d–e. It is important for students to realize that there are several ways to describe $\frac{3}{4}$:

$$\frac{3}{4} = \frac{1}{4} + \frac{1}{4} + \frac{1}{4},$$

$$\frac{3}{4} = \frac{1}{2} + \frac{1}{4},$$

$$\frac{3}{4} = \frac{1}{4} + \frac{1}{4} + \frac{1}{8} + \frac{1}{8},$$

$$\frac{3}{4} = \frac{1}{4} + \frac{1}{8} + \frac{1}{8} + \frac{1}{8} + \frac{1}{8},$$

$$\frac{3}{4} = \frac{1}{2} + \frac{1}{8} + \frac{1}{8}.$$

This will be discussed more explicitly in problems **10–12** in this section.

On the longest day of every year, the employees of Tut and Sons came together at a sacred place to honor Horus. Part of the sacred ritual involved turning a large wheel made from a heavy stone.

Every year, a young employee tried to turn the wheel as far as possible. No one, however, managed to turn the wheel the whole way around. After the wheel was turned part way, it slowly returned to its original position.

The wheel was always turned clockwise from its original position. A turn was considered complete when the handle was back at the "top." The pictures below show how far five different workers were able to turn the wheel from its original position.

8. Name the fraction of a whole turn shown on each wheel below. Use the Egyptian notation system to express each fraction.

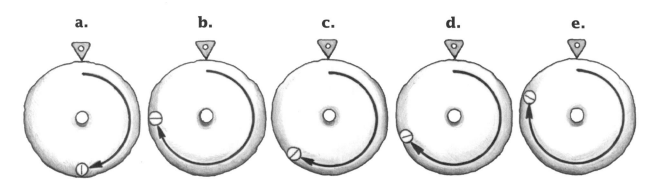

    a.   **b.**   **c.**   **d.**   **e.**

8. Notations may vary. Sample notations include the following:

a.

$(\frac{1}{2})$

b.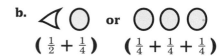

$(\frac{1}{2} + \frac{1}{4})$ $(\frac{1}{4} + \frac{1}{4} + \frac{1}{4})$

c.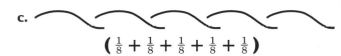

$(\frac{1}{8} + \frac{1}{8} + \frac{1}{8} + \frac{1}{8} + \frac{1}{8})$

or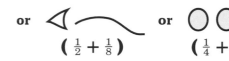

$(\frac{1}{2} + \frac{1}{8})$ $(\frac{1}{4} + \frac{1}{4} + \frac{1}{8})$

d.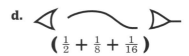

$(\frac{1}{2} + \frac{1}{8} + \frac{1}{16})$

or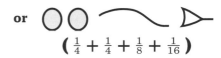

$(\frac{1}{4} + \frac{1}{4} + \frac{1}{8} + \frac{1}{16})$

e.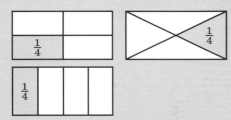

$(\frac{1}{2} + \frac{1}{4} + \frac{1}{16})$ $(\frac{1}{4} + \frac{1}{4} + \frac{1}{4} + \frac{1}{16})$

Overview Students examine circular diagrams that show different fractions of a whole turn. They use Egyptian symbols to describe what fraction of a whole turn is shown on each wheel.

About the Mathematics A wheel is a model of a fraction clock or fraction circle. This visual fraction model reinforces students' ideas about the relative magnitudes of different fractions. Students may more easily recognize fractional representations in a circle than in other shapes, such as rectangles.

For example, one-fourth of a circle always has the same identifiable shape.

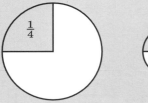

However, one-fourth of a rectangle can have different shapes, because of the different shapes of its parts or the different shapes of rectangles.

Planning Students can work in pairs or in small groups on problem **8.** Discuss problems **8d** and/or **8e** with students.

Comments about the Problems

8. The lack of any division marks on the wheels will force students to make appropriate subdivisions themselves. For example, in **8a,** the wheel is already divided into two halves. In **8b,** the wheel must be further subdivided into fourths to determine the fractional part past the $\frac{1}{2}$ turn ($\frac{1}{4}$). In **8c,** the wheel must be further subdivided into eighths to determine the fractional part past the $\frac{1}{2}$ turn ($\frac{1}{8}$).

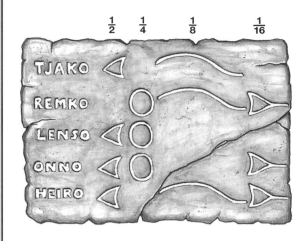

$\frac{1}{2}$ $\frac{1}{4}$ $\frac{1}{8}$ $\frac{1}{16}$

Each year, the accomplishment of the worker who turned the wheel was carved into a stone tablet. The tablet on the left shows workers' achievements for five different years.

9. **a.** How can you tell just by looking that Remko turned the wheel the shortest distance?

b. How can you tell just by looking which two workers turned the wheel the farthest?

c. List the workers in order, from the one who turned the wheel the farthest to the one who turned the wheel the shortest distance.

Back to Castor Oil

You can use symbols to express amounts of castor oil in different ways. For example, $1\frac{7}{8}$ pans of castor oil can be expressed in the following ways:

$1 + \frac{7}{8}$

$1 + \frac{1}{2} + \frac{3}{8}$

$1 + \frac{3}{4} + \frac{1}{8}$

$1 + \frac{1}{2} + \frac{1}{4} + \frac{1}{8}$

The employees of Tut and Sons preferred to use the fewest symbols possible because chiseling symbols into the stone was very hard work.

10. Which notation would they use to show $1\frac{7}{8}$ pans of castor oil?

11. On a separate piece of paper, record the amounts of oil shown on the right using as few symbols as possible.

12. Write rows of symbols for at least three different fractions. Then ask another student to simplify them.

a.

b.

c.

d.

9. a. His is the only name without a mark in the $\frac{1}{2}$ column.

b. Lenso and Onno, because their rows both start with $\frac{1}{2}$ and $\frac{1}{4}$

c. Onno
Lenso
Heiro
Tjako
Remko

10.

11. a.

b.

c.

d. /O

12. Symbol rows will vary.

Overview Students interpret the symbols on a stone tablet so that they can order and compare five workers' achievements in a wheel-turning ritual. In "Back to Castor Oil," students investigate how to use fewer fraction symbols to express amounts of oil more efficiently.

About the Mathematics The Egyptian symbols in problem **9** can be interpreted and compared in the same way as decimal numbers. You can first compare the symbols in the far left place, or in the second place if the symbols in the far left place are equal, and continue moving to the right to correctly order the numbers.

Planning Students may work individually or in pairs on these problems. You may assign problems **10–12** as homework.

Comments about the Problems

9. Students may use different strategies to solve this problem. For example, some students may use the same logic as that used in the Extension (on page 13 of the Teacher Guide) to reason as follows: Remko is the only one without a mark in the $\frac{1}{2}$ column, so he didn't turn the wheel $\frac{1}{2}$ turn. Therefore, all of his other fractions will not add up to one-half.

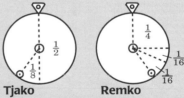

Tjako   Remko

Other students may determine the positions of the s/b wheel's handle and compare the distances. Or students may add the fractions for each worker to compare the distances. If so, they will find that Remko $= \frac{7}{16}$ turn, Tjako $= \frac{10}{16}$ turn, Heiro $= \frac{11}{16}$ turn, Lenso $= \frac{12}{16}$ turn, and Onno $= \frac{13}{16}$ turn.

c. The different strategies mentioned above can also be used to solve this problem.

10–12. Homework These problems may be assigned as homework. Students apply their knowledge of fractions to write sums of fractions in different ways.

12. Invite one student to write his or her notation on the board. Then have the rest of the class simplify it.

Refinement

Cleopatra and Daughters (C & D) was also a castor oil company. C & D improved the process of collecting castor oil and developed a new way to record the amount of oil they collected. The workers at Tut and Sons used the traditional Egyptian number system and refined their measurements by halving the units. The workers at C & D refined *their* measurements by dividing the units by ten.

Suppose C & D also applied their notation system to the sacred wheel. Their first step in refining measurements would be to divide the wheel into tenths, like the one on the right.

Each tenth of a turn can be represented by the fraction $\frac{1}{10}$. Two-tenths of a turn would be $\frac{2}{10}$. Cleopatra and Daughters used the symbol "–" to represent a tenth of a turn. Thus, two-tenths of a turn would be represented by "– –."

13. Represent the following turns in fractions and with the symbols used by C & D.

a.   **b.**   **c.**   **d.**

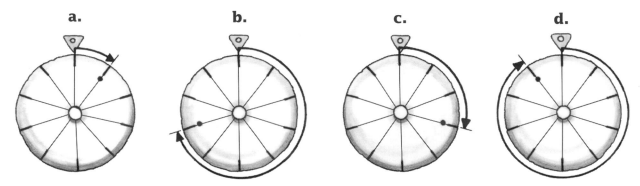

13. **a.** – $\left(\frac{1}{10}\right)$

   b. – – – – – – – $\left(\frac{7}{10}\right)$

   c. – – – $\left(\frac{3}{10}\right)$

   d. – – – – – – – – – $\left(\frac{9}{10}\right)$

Materials transparency showing a large circle divided into tenths, optional (one per class); overhead projector, optional (one per class)

Overview Students read about a different castor oil company and the way workers recorded the amounts of oil: refining their measurements by dividing the units by ten. Students describe a tenth of a turn of the wheel using a new symbol, a dash.

About the Mathematics A second number system, based on repeated division by 10 (the decimal system), is introduced. On the next page, the divisions of 10 (tenths) are divided again by ten.

Planning Students can work on problem **13** in pairs or in small groups.

Comments about the Problems

13. If students are having difficulty, you may want to prepare a transparency showing an enlarged version of the circle divided into tenths. This transparency may also be used to help students understand the problems on the next page.

After $\frac{1}{10}$, the next smaller unit shown on the wheel to the right would be $\frac{1}{10}$ of a tenth.

14. How many of these smaller units make one complete turn?

Each tenth of a tenth is one one-hundredth and can be expressed by the fraction $\frac{1}{100}$. C & D used the symbol "J" to represent one one-hundredth of a turn.

Example: _ _ _ JJJJJ

or

$\frac{3}{10} + \frac{5}{100}$

15. Represent the following turns using tenths and hundredths. Express your answers with the symbols used by C & D and with fractions.

a.

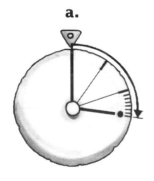

b.

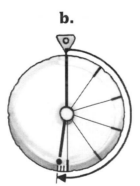

c.

d.

The next refinement would be a tenth of a tenth of a tenth. C & D used the symbol "ς" to represent this fraction.

16. How would you represent this fraction in our number system?

14. 100

15. a. $- - \text{♩♩♩♩♩♩♩}$ $(\frac{2}{10} + \frac{7}{100})$

   b. $- - - - - \text{♩♩♩}$ $(\frac{5}{10} + \frac{3}{100})$

   c. $- - - - \text{♩♩}$ $(\frac{4}{10} + \frac{2}{100})$

   d. $- - \text{♩♩♩♩}$ $(\frac{2}{10} + \frac{4}{100})$

16. $\frac{1}{1000}$

Materials transparency showing a large circle divided into tenths, optional (one per class); overhead projector, optional (one per class)

Overview Students divide a tenth of a wheel turn into tenths and learn that each tenth of a tenth is one one-hundredth. They then divide a hundredth of a wheel turn into tenths, thus discovering thousandths. They also learn the symbols that the C & D company used for hundredths and for thousandths.

About the Mathematics This number system is similar to the standard decimal system. However, it does not use the concept of place value. In the standard number system, zero is used to maintain the concept of place value, and the digits 0 through 9 have different values depending on their locations in numbers.

Planning You can use the transparency of the circle divided into tenths. Divide one-tenth of the circle into tenths to show the concept of hundredths. Students may work individually or in pairs on these problems. Discuss students' answers for problems **15** and **16.**

Comments about the Problems

16. If students have difficulty with this problem, you may want to ask them: *How many of these smaller units make up one-tenth?* [100] *And how many make up one complete turn?* [1,000]

The C & D company used this number system to log the number of pans of oil they collected. The symbol "Ω" represented one whole pan of oil. Below is the record that shows the amount of oil collected over seven days.

17. Write fractions for the symbols in the table on **Student Activity Sheet 1.** The first one has been done for you.

	Number of 1's	Number of $\frac{1}{10}$'s	Number of $\frac{1}{100}$'s	Number of $\frac{1}{1000}$'s	Number Expression ($1's + \frac{1}{10}'s + \frac{1}{100}'s + \frac{1}{1000}'s$)
a. ⌐ ⌐ ⌐ ⌐ J	0	3	1	0	$\frac{3}{10} + \frac{1}{100}$
b. ⌐ ⌐ ⌐ ⌐ ⌐ ⌐ ⌐ ⌐ ⌐					
c. J J J J					
d. Ω ⌐ ⌐ ⌐ ⌐ J J					
e. ϛϛϛϛϛ					
f. ⌐ ⌐ ⌐ ⌐ ⌐ J J ϛϛϛ					
g. Ω Ω ⌐ ⌐ ϛϛ					

18. Suppose you are an employee of C & D. Your job is to record the number of pans of oil that 10 workers have collected. Make up your own amounts for each of the 10 workers. Write them down using C & D notation. Use as few symbols as possible to express each amount. Exchange papers with classmates and have them make charts like the one above to find out how much oil was collected.

19. Suppose one worker collected Ω ⌐ ⌐ ⌐ J J J J J J ϛϛϛ pans of oil and another worker collected Ω Ω ⌐ ⌐ J J J J J ϛϛϛ pans. How many did they collect together? Write your answer using C & D notation.

17.

	Number of 1's	Number of $\frac{1}{10}$'s	Number of $\frac{1}{100}$'s	Number of $\frac{1}{1000}$'s	Number Expression (1's + $\frac{1}{10}$'s + $\frac{1}{100}$'s + $\frac{1}{1000}$'s)
a. ⎯ ⎯ ⎯ J	0	3	1	0	$\frac{3}{10} + \frac{1}{100}$
b. ⎯⎯⎯⎯⎯⎯⎯⎯	0	8	0	0	$\frac{8}{10}$
c. J J J J	0	0	4	0	$\frac{4}{100}$
d. Ω ⎯ ⎯ ⎯ J J	1	3	2	0	$1 + \frac{3}{10} + \frac{2}{100}$
e. ς ς ς ς ς ς	0	0	0	6	$\frac{6}{1000}$
f. ⎯ ⎯ ⎯ ⎯ J J ς ς	0	4	2	3	$\frac{4}{10} + \frac{2}{100} + \frac{3}{1000}$
g. Ω Ω ⎯ ⎯ ς ς	2	2	0	2	$2 + \frac{2}{10} + \frac{2}{1000}$

18. Amounts will vary.

19.

Ω	⎯ ⎯ ⎯	J J J J J J	ς ς ς
Ω Ω	⎯ ⎯	J J J J J	ς ς ς
Ω Ω Ω	⎯ ⎯ ⎯ ⎯ ⎯ ⎯	J	ς ς ς ς ς ς

Materials Student Activity Sheet 1 (one per student)

Overview Students use the C & D number system to express amounts of oil using tenths, hundredths, and thousandths of a pan. They then perform simple computations using the new system's symbolic notation.

About the Mathematics The table for problem **17** (Student Activity Sheet 1) will be used again in Section B, problem **13,** to develop the concept of place value—one of this unit's most important topics.

Planning After students have completed the table for problem **17,** you may want to use problem **18** for assessment. Students can work individually or in pairs on these problems.

Comments about the Problems

18. Informal Assessment This problem assesses students' understanding of place value and its use in ordering decimals.

19. Informal Assessment This problem assesses students' ability to estimate and compute with decimals. Students may not realize that $\frac{11}{100}$ is the same as $\frac{1}{10} + \frac{1}{100}$. This is acceptable at this point in the unit. This problem allows students to implicitly add decimals.

Interdisciplinary Connection You may want to remind students that the story is fictitious. Discuss the fact that the Egyptian number system (halving) was developed over 35 centuries ago, while division by 10 (the Hindu-Arabic number system) was not developed until the beginning of contemporary time, almost 20 centuries ago.

Summary

In order to make precise measurements, you need to use small measurement units. There are two well-known strategies for creating smaller units systematically:

- repeated division by two (halving)
- repeated division by 10

Egyptians used halving as a systematic approach to refining measurement. In our story, Cleopatra and Daughters' Castor Oil Company repeatedly divided by 10 to refine measurement.

Summary Questions

20. Tut & Sons' way of measuring with a dipstick is like using the measuring strip you made at the beginning of this section. Make a measuring strip that would work for Cleopatra and Daughters' smaller units.

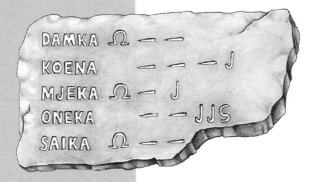

Years after the C & D Castor Oil Company closed, a tablet was found in the ruins. This tablet recorded oil production for five workers. Part of that tablet is shown on the left.

21. a. Can you tell who produced the most oil? Why or why not?

    b. Can you tell who produced the least oil? Why or why not?

    c. Other tablets mention that Saika was always the most productive worker. Show what the lost piece of the tablet would have looked like in order for this to be true.

22. Explain how a meter stick is related to C & D's measuring system.

20. Accept any measuring strip that is divided into 10 approximately equal divisions.

21. a. It is not possible to tell because Damka and Saika both produced $1\frac{2}{10}$ pans of oil. It is possible, however, that Saika produced more oil. The stone is broken where other symbols may have been chiseled in her record.

   b. Oneka definitely produced the least amount of oil. The symbols by Oneka's name show that he did not collect even one whole pan. Oneka's record also shows fewer $\frac{1}{10}$ symbols than Koena.

   c. Any additional symbol in the last row would mean that Saika produced the most oil.

22. A meter stick is a measurement strip repeatedly divided by ten. C + D's measuring system also repeatedly divided by ten to refine measurement.

Overview On this page, students review the two strategies for creating smaller measurement units that were explored in this section: repeated halving (division by two) and repeated division by 10.

Planning Students may work individually or in pairs on these problems. You may decide to use problems **20** and **21** for individual assessment. After students complete Section A, you may assign appropriate activities from the Try This! section, located on pages 37–40 of the Student Book, as homework.

Comments about the Problems

20–21. Informal Assessment These problems assess students' understanding of decimals as they relate to refinement in the measurement process.

   21. To solve this problem, students should use their knowledge of the symbols' values. This problem is similar to problem **9.** Students may reason using the number of symbols, as well as the value of each symbol.

   22. Students may notice this problem's similarity to problem **20**. A meter stick is a measurement strip repeatedly divided by tenths.

Work Students Do

By thinking of coins, such as pennies and dimes, as parts of a dollar, students make connections between amounts of money expressed as fractions and decimals. Students compare the prices of two different newspapers and write the prices in different ways. They express the values of different coin combinations both as decimals and fractional parts of a dollar. Students break down money amounts into hundreds of dollars, tens of dollars, dollars, dimes, and pennies to look at place value. They translate amounts of money expressed in fractions into dollar (decimal) notation. Students use a calculator to find fractions that are equivalent to common decimals. They also explore the relationship among fractions, decimals, and division notations.

Goals

Students will:

- understand the relationship between benchmark fractions and their decimal representations;

- use decimals in a context, such as money or measurement;

- estimate and compute with decimals;*

- understand place value and its use in ordering decimals;*

- use equivalent representations of fractions, decimals, and division notation.

  These goals are introduced in this section and are assessed in other sections in the unit.

Pacing

- approximately two 45-minute class sessions

Vocabulary

- decimal

- decimal point

- double number line

About the Mathematics

This section explores decimal number sense within the context of money. Changing the unit of measurement (for example, converting the amount expressed in dollars to cents) is a powerful strategy to help students understand decimal place value.

The preceding grade 5/6 unit, *Some of the Parts,* explored the relationship between division notation and fractions; now fractions and division notations are related to decimals. In the grade 5/6 unit *Per Sense,* the connection is made between all of the representations: division notation, fractions, decimals, and percents.

Materials

- Student Activity Sheets 1 and 2, pages 95 and 97 of the Teacher Guide (one of each per student)
- calculators, pages 39, 41, and 43 of the Teacher Guide (one per student)

Planning Instruction

It is assumed that students have had previous experience with money and will be able to apply this knowledge to explicit, important ideas about decimals. If you think students lack sufficient experience with money, you may want to review the names and values of coins, how money amounts are written using decimal points; and the numbers of pennies, nickels, dimes, and quarters in a dollar.

Students can work on problems 11–14 and 18 in pairs and on 15–17 in pairs or individually. They may work on the remaining problems in pairs or in small groups.

There are no optional problems in this section. Be sure to discuss problems 5, 8–10, 13, 14, and 18 with students.

Homework

You can assign problem 4 (page 32 of the Teacher Guide), problem 6 (page 34 of the Teacher Guide), and the Bringing Math Home activity (page 39 of the Teacher Guide) as homework. After students complete Section B, you may assign appropriate activities from the Try This! section, located on pages 37–40 of the *Measure for Measure* Student Book. The Try This! activities reinforce the key math concepts introduced in this section.

Planning Assessment

- Problems 7 and 14 can be used to informally assess students' understanding of the relationship between benchmark fractions and their decimal representations, and their ability to use equivalent representations of fractions, decimals, and division notation.
- Problem 16 can be used to informally assess students' ability to use equivalent representations of fractions, decimals, and division notation.
- Problem 19 can be used to informally assess students' ability to use equivalent representations of fractions, decimals, and division notation, and to use decimals in a context, such as money or measurement.

B. IT JUST MAKES CENTS

Quarters, Dimes, and Nickels

This picture shows two people reading different newspapers—the *News* and *Today's News*. The *News* costs $0.75 and *Today's News* costs 50 cents.

1. a. Which newspaper is more expensive?

   b. What is the difference in price?

2. Write the price of each newspaper in another way.

Bee Bop, a magazine about popular music, costs more in Canada. In the United States, it costs $2.25; in Canada, it costs $2.95.

3. Describe these prices in other ways.

The picture below shows several newspaper vending machines. The machines will take only quarters, dimes, and nickels.

4. Write as many different coin combinations as you can to pay for one $0.50 newspaper.

1. a. the *News*

   b. 25 cents, $0.25, or one quarter

2. Answer may vary. Sample answers:

   the News: 75 cents or $\frac{3}{4}$ dollar

   Today's News: $0.50 or $\frac{1}{2}$ dollar

3. Answer may vary. Sample answers:

   United States: 225 cents, $2\frac{1}{4}$ dollars, 2 dollars and 25 cents

   Canada: 2 dollars and 95 cents, almost 3 dollars, 295 cents

4. 2 quarters

   1 quarter, 2 dimes, 1 nickel

   1 quarter, 1 dime, 3 nickels

   1 quarter, 5 nickels

   5 dimes

   4 dimes, 2 nickels

   3 dimes, 4 nickels

   2 dimes, 6 nickels

   1 dime, 8 nickels

   10 nickels

Overview Students compare the prices of two newspapers, write the prices in different ways, and find different combinations of coins to make the same amount.

About the Mathematics In this section, students' implicit knowledge of decimals is expanded. Most students are able to work with decimals within the context of money. For example, students can read $0.89 as 89 cents, converting the original amount from dollars to cents.

Since working with integers is often easier than working with decimals, dollar amounts are often converted to cents to simplify computation. For example, consider the following problem: How much money will four hamburgers cost if each costs $0.89? To solve this problem, many students would add 89 + 89 + 89 + 89 to get 356 cents, and translate the total amount back to $3.56. This strategy is used throughout this section.

Planning If students lack sufficient experience with money, you may want to review each coin's name and value, the use of a decimal point to express amounts of money, and the number of pennies, nickels, dimes, and quarters in a dollar.

You might also begin with a short class discussion about money and encourage students to share any experiences they have had with foreign currency. Most foreign countries have a similar monetary system, with coins like nickels, dimes, and quarters.

Students can work in pairs or in small groups on problems **1–4.** You may ask them to finish problem **4** as homework.

Comments about the Problems

   1. b. Some students may write $0.25, but read the amount as *a quarter.*

   4. Homework This problem may be assigned as homework. You can ask students to share a few examples in class and then have them list other examples for homework.

Time for Change

This coin, a quarter, has a value of 25 cents. The name of this coin is the same as the name of the symbol $\frac{1}{4}$.

Because there are four quarters in one dollar, one quarter is $\frac{1}{4}$ of a dollar.

Because there are 10 dimes in one dollar, one dime is $\frac{1}{10}$ of a dollar.

Because there are one hundred cents in one dollar, one cent is $\frac{1}{100}$ of a dollar.

a. **b.**

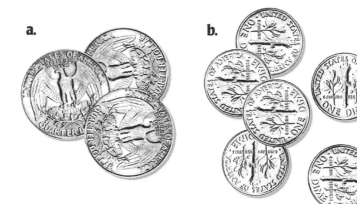

5. Write the values for the following amounts in two ways—with a dollar sign and with a fraction.

c.  **d.** **e.** **f.**

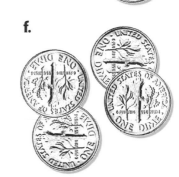

6. Describe or draw at least three other amounts. Write the value of each amount with a dollar sign and with a fraction.

The dot in $0.50 is called the **decimal point,** and 0.50 is called a **decimal**. Money can help you see relationships between decimals and common fractions:

$$0.50 = \frac{50}{100} \text{ (50 pennies)} \qquad 0.50 = \frac{2}{4} \text{ (two quarters)}$$

If a decimal ends with a zero, the zero is sometimes omitted (for example, 0.50 = 0.5). If the decimal refers to money, the ending zero is usually kept.

5. The form of the fraction may vary. Possible answers:

   a. $0.75 $\frac{3}{4}$ or $\frac{75}{100}$

   b. $0.60 $\frac{60}{100}$ or $\frac{6}{10}$

   c. $0.25 $\frac{1}{4}$ or $\frac{25}{100}$

   d. $0.10 $\frac{1}{10}$ or $\frac{10}{100}$

   e. $0.03 $\frac{3}{100}$

   f. $0.40 $\frac{40}{100}$ or $\frac{4}{10}$

6. Answers will vary. However, they should look similar to those for problem **5.**

Overview Students express the values of different coin combinations as decimals (using dollar signs) and as fractions.

About the Mathematics One the goals of this section is for students to understand and use equivalent benchmark fractions and decimals. On this page, the relationships between decimals and fractions is made explicit. For example, students learn that $0.25 = one quarter $= \frac{1}{4}$ of a dollar.

Planning Students may work on problems **5** and **6** in pairs or in small groups. After students solve problem **5**, discuss their solutions with the whole class. Problem **6** may be assigned as homework.

Comments about the Problems

  5. Some students may express fractions in their simplest forms, while others may not. This difference may be due to the way individual students perceive the monetary relationships. For example, some students may think of $0.10 as 10 cents out of a dollar and write $\frac{10}{100}$, while others may think of one dime as a tenth of a dollar and write $\frac{1}{10}$. Consider both answers correct. You may want to discuss the connection between the name and the value of one *cent*.

  6. Homework This problem may be assigned as homework. Students may come up with amounts of money larger than one dollar.

Did You Know? A cent is one one-hundredth of a dollar. *Cent* is the French word for "hundred."

For 50 cents, you can also write $\frac{2}{4}$ dollar or $\frac{50}{100}$, although you probably will not find these notations in signs or advertisements. Can you guess why?

7. As shown above, there are many possible fractions that express a given decimal. Make a list of several other decimals. Then write fractions that express each decimal you have listed.

$135.45

$100.00	$10.00	$1.00	$0.10	$0.01

$0.85

$100.00	$10.00	$1.00	$0.10	$0.01

If you buy something that costs $4.32, you might pay with 4 dollars, 3 dimes, and 2 pennies. Or you might pay with 4 dollars, 2 dimes, and 12 pennies.

8. Copy the table on the left. Write four different ways to pay $135.45 using only $100 bills, $10 bills, $1 bills, dimes, and pennies. Do the same for $0.85.

You can also express ways to pay in fractions of dollars.

For example, $135.45 $= 135 + \frac{4}{10} + \frac{5}{100}$ or $135 + \frac{2}{10} + \frac{25}{100}$.

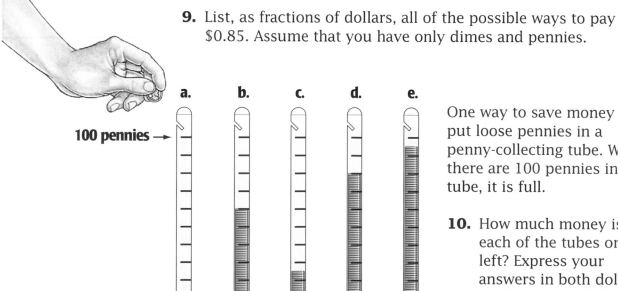

100 pennies →

9. List, as fractions of dollars, all of the possible ways to pay $0.85. Assume that you have only dimes and pennies.

a.   **b.**   **c.**   **d.**   **e.**

One way to save money is to put loose pennies in a penny-collecting tube. When there are 100 pennies in the tube, it is full.

10. How much money is in each of the tubes on the left? Express your answers in both dollars and fractions of dollars.

7. Answers will vary. Possible answers:

$0.75 = \frac{3}{4}$ $0.25 = \frac{1}{4}$ $0.40 = \frac{40}{100}$

$0.60 = \frac{6}{10}$ $0.03 = \frac{3}{100}$

8. Answers will vary. Possible answers:

	$100.00	$10.00	$1.00	$0.10	$0.01
$135.45	1	3	5	4	5
		13	5	4	5
			135	4	5
				1354	5

	$100.00	$10.00	$1.00	$0.10	$0.01
$0.85				8	5
				7	15
				6	25
					85

9. $0.85 = \frac{85}{100}$

$\frac{8}{10} + \frac{5}{100}$ $\frac{4}{10} + \frac{45}{100}$

$\frac{7}{10} + \frac{15}{100}$ $\frac{3}{10} + \frac{55}{100}$

$\frac{6}{10} + \frac{25}{100}$ $\frac{2}{10} + \frac{65}{100}$

$\frac{5}{10} + \frac{35}{100}$ $\frac{1}{10} + \frac{75}{100}$

10. a. $0.10 $\frac{1}{10}$

b. $0.60 $\frac{6}{10}$

c. $0.25 $\frac{2}{10} + \frac{5}{100}$, or $\frac{25}{100}$

d. $0.80 $\frac{8}{10}$

e. $0.95 $\frac{9}{10} + \frac{5}{100}$, or $\frac{95}{100}$

Overview Students break money amounts into hundreds of dollars, tens of dollars, dollars, dimes, and cents to look at place value. They express different monetary amounts as dollars and fractions of dollars.

About the Mathematics By now students should know the decimal monetary amounts of $0.10, $0.25, $0.50, $0.75, $0.80 and their fractional equivalents. You may use a *double number line* to help students see the relationships between these fraction and decimal equivalents:

$.10	$.25	$.50	$.75	$.80	$1.00
$\frac{1}{10}$	$\frac{1}{4}$	$\frac{1}{2}$	$\frac{3}{4}$	$\frac{8}{10}$	$\frac{1}{1}$

List the monetary amounts along the top of the number line and ask students which coins can be used to express each amount. Then ask students to write the corresponding fractions along the bottom of the number line. For example, a dime links $0.10 to $\frac{1}{10}$ of a dollar.

Planning Problem **7** can be used as an assessment. Students can work in pairs or in small groups on problems **8–10**. Be sure to discuss students' solutions to these problems.

Comments about the Problems

7. Informal Assessment This problem assesses students' understanding of the relationship between benchmark fractions and their decimal representations, and their ability to use equivalent representations of fractions, decimals, and division notation.

8. You may ask the students to think about the system used by the C & D Castor Oil Company in Section A as they work on this problem.

9. If students are having difficulty, suggest that they make a table similar to the one in problem **8.** They can also use their knowledge of equivalent coins and fractions.

10. Observe whether or not students express their answers only in terms of hundredths of a dollar. If so, encourage them to write other combinations of fractions of a dollar.

11. Sue, Jamal, and James decided to collect money from other Drama Club members so that they could buy their drama coach a birthday present. Sue collected $12.06; Jamal collected $13.04; and James collected $10.20.

   a. Use paper and pencil to find the total they collected.

   b. Now use your calculator to find the total.

   c. Are your answers to parts **a** and **b** the same? Explain.

12. Below are three dollar amounts expressed as fractions. Which one is easiest to write as dollars? Explain your answer.

   a. $3 + \frac{1}{2} + \frac{3}{4}$

   b. $3 + \frac{2}{10} + \frac{6}{100}$

   c. $3 + \frac{3}{10} + \frac{14}{100}$

13. Look at the chart you made on **Student Activity Sheet 1.** Compare it to the relationships that you have discovered among fractions, decimals, and money. Describe this comparison.

Activity

Money amounts are not the only things that are usually written as decimals rather than as fractions. Many calculators display decimals instead of fractions. Some decimal numbers, however, are easily associated with fractions. For instance, from the activities in this unit, you know that 0.25 is $\frac{1}{4}$.

14. Use your calculator to find other decimals that can easily be written as fractions.

11. a. $35.30

    b. The answer displayed on the calculator was 35.3.

    c. Yes. If you do the computation by hand, the answer will be 35.30. The difference is the last zero.

12. Dollar amount **b** is easiest to express in dollar notation because of its place-value notation. Both **a** and **c** require translation to other forms before they can be written in dollar notation.

    a. $3 + \frac{1}{2} + \frac{3}{4} = 3 + \frac{1}{2} + \frac{2}{4} + \frac{1}{4}$

           $= 3 + \frac{1}{2} + \frac{1}{2} + \frac{1}{4}$

           $= 3 + 1 + \frac{1}{4}$

           $= \$4.25$

    b. $3 + \frac{2}{10} + \frac{6}{100} = \$3.26$

    c. $3 + \frac{3}{10} + \frac{14}{100} = 3 + \frac{3}{10} + \frac{1}{10} + \frac{4}{100} = \$3.44$

13. Answers may vary. However, students should note that the place value is the same in each situation.

14. Answers will vary. Possible answers:

    $0.75 = \frac{3}{4}$

    $0.1 = \frac{1}{10}$

    $0.5 = \frac{1}{2}$

    $0.01 = \frac{1}{100}$

Materials Student Activity Sheet 1 (one per student), calculators (one per student)

Overview Students compare the sum total found using paper and pencil to the one obtained using a calculator. They learn that if a decimal number ends in zero, a calculator will not display the last zero. Students then translate dollar amounts expressed as fractions into their decimal equivalents. Students also use a calculator to find fractions that are equivalent to common decimals.

About the Mathematics Problem **11** introduces the concept of insignificant zeros. If a decimal number ends with a zero, a calculator will not display the last zero. This concept will be extended in Section C.

Planning Students can work on problems **11–14** in pairs. Discuss students' solutions to problems **13** and **14**.

Comments about the Problems

    11. Some students may line up the numbers and add, while others may convert the dollar amounts into fractions, add, and then translate the answer to a decimal amount.

    12. In this problem, students informally add decimals.

    13. This problem explicitly addresses place value.

    14. Informal Assessment This problem assesses students' understanding of the relationship between benchmark fractions and their decimal representations, and their ability to use equivalent representations of fractions, decimals, and division notation.

    If students are having difficulty using the calculator to find decimal-fraction relationships, suggest that they express each fraction using division notation and key enter the sequence. For example, to find the decimal equivalent for $\frac{2}{5}$, express the fraction using division notation $[2 \div 5]$. Enter this key sequence on the calculator. The result is 0.4.

Bringing Math Home Ask students to look through newspapers and magazines with a family member to find headlines and articles in which decimals and fractions are used. Have students discuss why the fraction or decimal representation was chosen in each case.

Fractions are useful in measurement. They are also useful in division. For example:

Two children share one submarine sandwich equally. Each child gets $\frac{1}{2}$ of a sandwich.

or

Four students share three dollars equally. Each student gets $\frac{3}{4}$ of a dollar, or 75 cents.

15. Create three division problems for which the answers are fractions.

16. Use your calculator, your number sense, and **Student Activity Sheet 2** to complete the table on the right.

17. Solve the following fraction problems by changing fractions to decimals, adding the decimals, and then changing the answers back into fractions. You may use your calculator.

Division	Decimal	Fraction
6 ÷ 12		
	0.25	
		$\frac{7}{10}$
		$\frac{1}{8}$
3 ÷ 4		
	0.1	
		$\frac{2}{5}$

a. $\frac{1}{2}$ + $\frac{1}{4}$ __?__ + __?__ = __?__ = __?__

b. $\frac{3}{4}$ + $\frac{3}{4}$ __?__ + __?__ = __?__ = __?__

c. $\frac{3}{4}$ + $\frac{1}{2}$ __?__ + __?__ = __?__ = __?__

d. $\frac{1}{10}$ + $\frac{1}{5}$ __?__ + __?__ = __?__ = __?__

15. Problems will vary. However, they will probably be similar to the examples on page 17 of the Student Book.

16.

Division	Decimal	Fraction
6 ÷ 12	0.5	$\frac{1}{2}$
1 ÷ 4	0.25	$\frac{1}{4}$
7 ÷ 10	0.7	$\frac{7}{10}$
1 ÷ 8	0.125	$\frac{1}{8}$
3 ÷ 4	0.75	$\frac{3}{4}$
1 ÷ 10	0.1	$\frac{1}{10}$
2 ÷ 5	0.4	$\frac{2}{5}$

17. a. $0.5 + 0.25 = 0.75 = \frac{3}{4}$

  b. $0.75 + 0.75 = 1.5 = 1\frac{1}{2}$

  c. $0.75 + 0.5 = 1.25 = 1\frac{1}{4}$

  d. $0.1 + 0.2 = 0.3 = \frac{3}{10}$

Materials Student Activity Sheet 2 (one per student), calculators (one per student)

Overview Students make a table showing the relationships among division notation, decimals, and fractions. They create division problems for which the answers are fractions.

About the Mathematics Fractions can be the result of a measurement, as in the castor oil problems in Section A; they can also be the result of a division computation, as shown here. In relating fractions, decimals, and division notation, students may recall the context of dividing submarine sandwiches from the grade 5/6 unit *Some of the Parts*. It is important for students to develop their own strategies for solving problems with fractions and decimals.

Planning Some students may need to be reminded about the correct key sequence to use when computing division using a calculator. For example, to compute 12 ÷ 2 using a calculator, students must
• press the one and two keys (12),
• press the division symbol key (÷),
• press the two key (2), and
• press the equal sign key (=).

Students may work in pairs or individually on problems **15–17.** You may use problem **16** as an assessment.

Comments about the Problems

15. Remind students also to write the fractions that are involved in their division problems.

16. Informal Assessment This problem assesses students' ability to use equivalent representations of fractions, decimals, and division notation. It may help students to think about the relationships in terms of money. For example, 6 ÷ 12 can be thought of as $6.00 divided among 12 people, which would result in $0.50 per person.

17. Some students may express their answers in tenths or hundredths, while others may use fourths or halves. Discuss students' reasoning. For example, some students may see 0.75 as money (three quarters) and write $\frac{3}{4}$. Others may think of 0.75 in terms of place value(7 tenths and 5 hundredths) and write $\frac{75}{100}$ Accept either answer as correct. Do not require students to express fractions in their simplest form.

Common relationships between fractions and decimals include:

$$\tfrac{1}{10} = 0.1 \qquad \tfrac{1}{4} = 0.25 \qquad \tfrac{1}{2} = 0.5 \qquad \tfrac{3}{4} = 0.75$$

18. Use your calculator to extend the above list.

Summary

Money amounts are often written with two digits following the decimal point. The two digits after the decimal point may be read as cents. For example, $1.25 may be read as "one dollar and 25 cents."

Because one cent equals $\tfrac{1}{100}$ dollar, $1.25 can also be read as $1 + \tfrac{25}{100}$ dollar, and $1.25 = 1 + \tfrac{25}{100}$, or $1 + \tfrac{2}{10} + \tfrac{5}{100}$.

In this section, you used money to study relationships between decimals and fractions.

Some common relationships are:

$$0.25 = \tfrac{1}{4} \quad \text{(a quarter)}$$
$$0.50 = \tfrac{1}{2} \quad \text{(a half-dollar)}$$
$$0.75 = \tfrac{3}{4} \quad \text{(three quarters)}$$
$$0.10 = \tfrac{1}{10} \quad \text{(a dime)}$$
$$0.01 = \tfrac{1}{100} \quad \text{(a penny)}$$

You can always change a fraction into a decimal by dividing. If a decimal ends with zeros, the zeros are sometimes omitted (for example, 34.50 = 34.5). If the decimals refer to money, the ending zero is usually kept.

Summary Questions

19. a. Express $0.60 as a fraction of a dollar.
  b. Express $0.60 as a decimal.
  c. Express $0.60 as a fraction.
  d. Express $0.60 as a division problem.

18. Answers will vary. Possible answers:

$\frac{1}{8}$ = 0.125

$\frac{2}{5}$ = 0.4

$\frac{1}{100}$ = 0.01

19. a. $\frac{3}{5}$, $\frac{6}{10}$, or $\frac{60}{100}$

b. 0.60

c. $\frac{60}{100}$, $\frac{3}{5}$, or $\frac{6}{10}$

d. 3 ÷ 5; $3 divided by five people

Materials calculators (one per student)

Overview Students use their calculators to convert fractions to decimals. They also read the Summary, which reviews the most important relationships between fractions and decimals:
• one quarter = $\frac{1}{4}$ of a dollar or $0.25
• one half-dollar = $\frac{1}{2}$ of a dollar or $0.50
• three quarters = $\frac{3}{4}$ of a dollar or $0.75
• one dime = $\frac{1}{10}$ of a dollar or $0.10
• one penny = $\frac{1}{100}$ of a dollar or $0.01

Finally, students express an amount of money as a fraction of a dollar, as a decimal, and as a division problem.

Planning Students can work on problem **18** in pairs or in small groups. Discuss this problem and the Summary with the whole class. You may use problem **19** as an assessment. After students complete Section B, you may assign appropriate activities from the Try This! section, located on pages 37–40 of the Student Book, as homework.

Comments about the Problems

18. If students are having difficulty computing division using their calculators, you may need to review the correct key sequence. See the Planning section on page 41 of this Teacher Guide.

19. Informal Assessment This problem assesses students' ability to use equivalent representations of fractions, decimals, and division notation, and to use decimals in a context such as money or measurement.

SECTION C. SPORTING DECIMALS

Work Students Do

Students use their knowledge about decimals within different sports contexts. They read and interpret decimals that refer to times in a 200-meter race, scores in basketball, and distances in a long jump competition. Students compute with decimals to learn about record holders for the men's long jump. They also measure a distance equal to Mike Powell's record jump and compare that distance to the width of their classroom. Students use decimals to describe a distance that is between two other distances. They match a picture of the finish of a track race with the runners' given times. Students use and interpret decimal numbers that represent cycling distances measured in kilometers.

Goals

Students will:

- use decimals in a context, such as money or measurement;

- estimate and compute with decimals;

- understand place value and its use in ordering decimals;

- understand the metric system and its relationship to decimals;

- understand decimals as they relate to refinement in the measurement process;*

- represent and use decimals in a variety of equivalent forms to solve problems in real-world and mathematical situations;

- choose an appropriate visual model or strategy to represent and solve problems involving decimals.

  This goal is assessed in Sections A and D of this unit.

Pacing

- approximately two 45-minute class sessions

Vocabulary

- centimeter
- decimeter
- kilometer
- meter
- millimeter
- number line

About the Mathematics

In this section, decimal place value, comparing and ordering decimals, and doing simple decimal computations are emphasized within a given context.

The *number line* is introduced as a model to order and compare decimals within the context of a long jump. This model was also used in Section A in a different format in the "Cleopatra & Daughters" activities.

In previous sections, students changed decimal units of measure by changing dollar amounts into cents. That strategy is not always applicable when working with decimals that represent metric units of length, such as millimeters, so a more formal way to change measurement units within the metric system is introduced here.

Materials

- meter sticks or metric measuring tapes, pages 47, 49, and 51 of the Teacher Guide (one per pair of students)
- local newspapers, page 57 of the Teacher Guide (about six copies per class)

Planning Instruction

Many students will be familiar with the different sports contexts in this section, but be sensitive to those students who are not. You can either explain a context or substitute a more familiar one.

Have copies of your local newspaper available, especially the sports section. Encourage students to find decimals used in the articles. They can share their understanding of the meanings of the decimals used within the newspaper articles with other students.

This section uses the metric system of measurement in several contexts. Since some students may be unfamiliar with the metric system, you might briefly discuss the meaning of centimeters, meters, and kilometers. If possible, demonstrate how to read and use a meter stick or metric measuring tape. You might also have students measure the length of common classroom objects with meter sticks or metric measuring tapes.

They may work on most of the problems in this section in pairs or in small groups. You may want students to work on problems 15 and 16 in pairs or individually. Be sure to discuss students' solutions and strategies for problems 10, 11, and 17–19.

Problem 14 is optional.

Homework

You can assign problem 20 (page 56 of the Teacher Guide) as homework. You may also assign the Extensions (pages 53 and 57 of the Teacher Guide) and the Writing Opportunity (page 57 of the Teacher Guide) as homework. After students complete Section C, you may assign appropriate activities from the Try This! section, located on pages 37–40 of the *Measure for Measure* Student Book. The Try This! activities reinforce the key math concepts introduced in this section.

Planning Assessment

- Problem 2 can be used to informally assess students' ability to use decimals in a context, such as money or measurement, and their understanding of place value and its use in ordering decimals.
- Problem 15 can be used to informally assess students' understanding of place value and its use in ordering decimals, and their ability to choose an appropriate visual model or strategy to represent and solve problems involving decimals.
- Problem 16 can be used to informally assess students' ability to estimate and compute with decimals, and to choose an appropriate visual model or strategy to represent and solve problems involving decimals. It also assesses their understanding of place value and its use in ordering decimals.
- Problem 20 can be used to informally assess students' ability to use decimals in a context, such as money or measurement, and to represent and use decimals in a variety of equivalent forms to solve problems in real-world and mathematical situations. It also assesses their understanding of the metric system and its relationship to decimals and their understanding of place value and its use in ordering decimals.

C. SPORTING DECIMALS

Sports Numbers

Gwen Torrence at the 1992 Summer Olympics in Barcelona, Spain.

Decimals are used in sports, but not always in the same way. For example, sometimes they refer to time, sometimes to scores, and sometimes to distances.

1. Look at the following numbers and explain what each one means.

Time	Score	Distance
Gwen Torrence ran the 200-meter dash in 21.81 seconds.	J. R. Rider averaged 29.1 points per game.	Jackie Joyner-Kersee jumped 7.07 meters.

You can describe a decimal in many different ways. For example, Gwen Torrence ran 200 meters in:

21.81 seconds *or*

just under 22 seconds *or*

between 21 and 22 seconds *or*

a little over 21 seconds *or*

$21 + \frac{8}{10} + \frac{1}{100}$ seconds.

2. Describe the other two examples, 29.1 points and 7.07 meters, in different ways.

Prospective Bucks Picks

Here is a list of the statistics for the 1992–93 season for players who might be available when the Milwaukee Bucks pick in Wednesday's draft:

Player, Pos., School	Ht.	Wt.	Pts.	Reb.	Ast.
Rodney Rogers, F, Wake Forest	6-7	235	21.2	7.4	2.3
J.R. Rider, G/F, UNVL	6-5	215	29.1	8.9	2.5
Calbert Cheaney, F, Indiana	6-7	209	22.4	6.3	2.4
Acie Earl, C, Iowa	6-10	240	16.9	8.8	1.3
Vin Baker, C, Hartford	6-11	232	28.3	10.7	1.9
Allan Houston, G, Tennessee	6-6	200	22.3	4.8	3.0
Bobby Hurley, G, Duke	6-0	165	17.0	2.6	8.2

Source: Wisconsin State Journal.

WOMEN'S 200 METERS / August 6

RANK	CTRY	ATHLETE	TIME
1	USA	Gwen Torrence	21.81
2	JAM	Juliet Cuthbert	22.02
3	JAM	Merlene Ottey	22.09
4	EUN	Irina Privalova	22.19
5	USA	Carlette Guidry-White	22.30
6	JAM	Grace Jackson Small	22.58
7	USA	Michelle Finn	22.61
8	EUN	Galina Malchugina	22.63

WOMEN'S LONG JUMP / August 7

RANK	CTRY	ATHLETE	METERS	FT/IN
1	GER	Heike Drechsler	7.14	23–5¼
2	EUN	Inessa Kravets	7.12	23–4½
3	USA	Jackie Joyner-Kersee	7.07	23–2½
4	LTU	N. Medvedera	6.76	22–2
5	ROM	M. Dulgheru	6.71	22–0
6	EUN	I. Muchailova	6.68	21–11
7	USA	Sharon Couch	6.66	21–10¼
8	USA	Sheila Echols	6.62	21–8¾

1. Answers will vary. Possible answers:

Time:

- 21 seconds and $\frac{81}{100}$ of a second

- 21 seconds, eight tenths, and one-hundredth of a second

- 21 seconds, and $\frac{8}{10}$ and $\frac{1}{100}$ of a second

- almost 22 seconds

Score:

- 29 points and $\frac{1}{10}$ of a point

- 29 points and one-tenth of a point

- 20 points, 9 points, and $\frac{1}{10}$ of a point

- a little less than 30 points

Distance:

- 7 meters and $\frac{7}{100}$ of a meter

- 7 meters and 7 centimeters

- 707 centimeters

- 7 meters, and $\frac{0}{10}$ and $\frac{7}{100}$ of a meter

- about 7 meters or a little over 7 meters

2. Answers will vary. Possible answers:

29.1 is about 29 points, between 29 and 30 points, $29 + \frac{1}{10}$ points, $29\frac{10}{100}$ points, or $20 + 9 + \frac{1}{10}$ points

7.07 is about 7.0 meters, between 7 and 8 meters, 7 meters and 7 centimeters, $7\frac{7}{100}$ meters, or $7 + \frac{7}{100}$ meters

Materials meter sticks, optional (one per class)

Overview Students use their knowledge about decimals within different sports contexts. They interpret decimal numbers that refer to times in a women's 200-meter race, average points in basketball, and distances in a women's long jump competition.

About the Mathematics In Section B, students solved decimal problems by changing dollars into quarters or cents (by changing the unit of measurement). Such a strategy is not applicable here, so a more formal method for changing decimals within the metric system is introduced. Decimal place value and comparing and ordering decimals are also emphasized in this section.

Students need not use specific algorithms at this point. It is important for them to develop their own problem-solving strategies.

The metric measurement system is used throughout the *Mathematics in Context* curriculum. If students are not familiar with metric units, such as centimeters and meters, it might be helpful to show them how to read and use a meter stick and allow them to measure classroom objects. However, you need not spend a lot of time discussing metric measurement units, because they will be revisited in other units.

Planning You may introduce this section with a short class discussion about students' sports experiences. Some students may know their personal records (in times or distances). You may use problem **2** as an assessment.

Comments about the Problems

1. Some students may describe the numbers by rounding them; they may say that 21.81 seconds is about 22 seconds. Others may use their knowledge of decimals, fractions, and place value. For example, a student might express 21.81 seconds as 21 seconds, $\frac{8}{10}$ and $\frac{1}{100}$ of a second. Both descriptions are acceptable.

2. **Informal Assessment** This problem assesses students' ability to use decimals in a context, such as money or measurement, and their understanding of place value and its use in ordering decimals.

Students should describe the decimal numbers both ways: by estimating and by giving an exact answer using whole numbers and fractions.

Long Jump

In international track competitions, distances in the long jump event are measured in **meters (m).**

A meter can be divided into **centimeters (cm).**
One meter is equal to 100 centimeters.

A meter can also be divided into **decimeters (dm).**
One meter is equal to 10 decimeters.

The chart on the right shows past world records for the men's long jump.

3. Which record stood the longest?

4. Jesse Owens set a new world record in 1935. How much farther did he jump than Peter O'Connor in 1901?

5. Did anyone break a world record by more meters than Jesse Owens did in 1935?

Record Holders		
1901	Peter O'Connor (Great Britain)	7.61 m
1921	Edwin Gourdin (USA)	7.69 m
1924	Robert LeGendre (USA)	7.76 m
1925	William de Hart Hubbard (USA)	7.89 m
1928	Edward Hamm (USA)	7.90 m
1928	Sylvio Cator (Haiti)	7.93 m
1931	Chuhei Nambu (Japan)	7.98 m
1935	Jesse Owens (USA)	8.13 m
1960	Ralph Boston (USA)	8.21 m
1961	Ralph Boston (USA)	8.24 m
1961	Ralph Boston (USA)	8.28 m
1962	Igor Ter-Ovanesyan (USSR)	8.31 m
1964	Ralph Boston (USA)	8.31 m
1964	Ralph Boston (USA)	8.34 m
1965	Ralph Boston (USA)	8.35 m
1967	Igor Ter-Ovanesyan (USSR)	8.35 m
1968	Bob Beamon (USA)	8.90 m
1991	Mike Powell (USA)	8.95 m

Activity

Ask your teacher for a meter stick or a measuring tape at least one meter long. See if you can take steps that are about one meter long.

6. Using one-meter steps, pace off the distance of Mike Powell's jump.

7. Use a meter stick or measuring tape to measure (as precisely as possible) the distance that Mike Powell jumped and compare it to your estimation from problem **6.**

8. Compare the length of Mike Powell's jump to the width of your classroom.

9. Express the length of Mike Powell's jump in centimeters.

3. Jesse Owens's record stood the longest.

4. Jesse Owens extended the record by 0.52 meter (8.13 − 7.61).

5. Yes. Bob Beeman broke the record by 0.55 meter (8.90 − 8.35).

6. Students should pace off approximately 9 meters.

7. A meter stick should give a more precise measurement.

8. Answers will vary according to the width of the classroom.

9. 895 centimeters

Materials meter sticks or metric measuring tapes (one per pair of students)

Overview Students learn about the metric unit *meter* and how one meter can be subdivided into *centimeter* and *decimeter* units. Students use decimals to investigate world record distances for the men's long jump competition. They also pace off and measure Mike Powell's record long jump and compare that distance to the width of the classroom.

About the Mathematics The context of the long jump is used to introduce the number line as a model for decimals. Similarly, the wheel model used in Section A can be seen as a circular number line from zero to one.

The metric measurement context lays the foundation for using a horizontal or vertical number line as a model to estimate decimals, understand decimal place value, and convert between different metric units.

Planning Students may work on problems **3–9** in pairs or in small groups.

Comments about the Problems

4. One strategy used in simple decimal computations is changing the unit of measurement. In this problem, some students may change meters into centimeters (8.13 m = 813 cm and 7.61 m = 761 cm) and then subtract to find the answer (813 − 761 = 52 cm).

If students are having difficulty, encourage them to estimate an answer. Estimating may help them find a strategy for determining a more accurate answer.

6–9. This activity is probably best done outside or in a hallway or gymnasium. The purpose of the activity is to give students an understanding of the actual lengths of one meter and one centimeter.

If your average student's pace is considerably shorter than one meter, skip problem **6**.

Depending on where you do this activity, you may ask students to solve problem **14** on page 21 of the Student Book at the same time. In this problem, students measure the distance they can jump in centimeters.

To make more precise measurements, you can use units that are smaller than centimeters. Find these units on a metric measuring tape. The smaller units are called *millimeters.*

10. a. How many millimeters are in a meter?

   b. How many millimeters are in a centimeter?

11. a. What decimal describes the distance between 2.37 meters and 2.38 meters?

   b. Write a decimal that is between 2.37 and 2.38, but closer to 2.38.

Below is a diagram of the measuring stick by the jump pit of a track. The markers indicate the distances in meters.

12. How far did this athlete jump? (Long jump distances are measured to the heel print of the athlete.)

13. Did this athlete jump farther than Jesse Owens in 1935?

14. a. Measure how far you can jump in centimeters.

   b. Compare the distance of your jump with the distances of your classmates' jumps.

   c. Is it true that taller people can jump farther than shorter people?

10. a. There are 1,000 millimeters in a meter.

    b. There are 10 millimeters in a centimeter.

11. a. 0.01 meter

    b. Answers will vary between 2.375 and 2.37$\overline{9}$.

12. about 8.5 meters

13. Yes, Jesse Owens jumped 8.13 meters, while this athlete jumped about 8.5 meters.

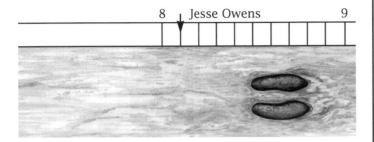

14. a. Answers will vary depending on the length of the jump.

    b. Comparisons will vary. Encourage students to determine who jumped the farthest.

    c. Answers will vary. There are several factors other than height that could affect the distance a person is able to jump. For example, a person's technique or style (using arms, toes, etc.) or his or her strength could affect the distance.

Materials meter sticks or metric measuring tapes (one per pair of students)

Overview Students are introduced to the metric unit *millimeter* on this page. They use decimals to describe a distance between two given distances. Students use a drawing of a meter stick without subdivisions to estimate distances. They also measure and compare distances they have jumped.

Planning You may want to begin with a short class discussion about the metric units that have been used so far: meter, decimeter, and centimeter. Then discuss how a centimeter can be subdivided into millimeters. You can refer students to the refinement of measurement as used in the "Cleopatra & Daughters" problems, in which a tenth was refined by dividing it into tenths.

Students can work on problems **10–14** in pairs or in small groups. Have students discuss their solutions and strategies for problems **10** and **11** before they continue to work on problems **13** and **14**. Problem **14** is optional.

Comments about the Problems

10. Students should understand that a millimeter is one-tenth of a centimeter.

    You may point out that the prefix *milli* means "one-thousandth" and that it refers to one-thousandth of a meter. Similarly, the prefix *centi* means "one-hundredth" and refers to one-hundredth of a meter.

11. Discuss students' strategies for finding the answer, 0.01 meter. Ask students to determine how 0.01 meter can be expressed using other metric units [0.01 meter = 0.1 decimeter = 1 centimeter = 10 millimeters].

    By frequently referring to the relationships between decimals as expressed in different metric units, students will develop a better understanding of the metric system and the place values of the decimal digits.

12. Students may see that the jump is halfway between 8 and 9 meters. The total distance of the jump is measured from the beginning of the jump pit to the heel print of the jumper.

14. If students did not complete the activity on page 20 of the Student Book, allow them to do so now, or you may skip this problem entirely. See the comments for problems **6–9** on page 49 of the Teacher Guide.

Sprints

The 1992 Summer Olympics were held in Barcelona, Spain. Below are the medal-winning times for two of the women's races.

200 meters		400 meters	
Gwen Torrence USA	21.81 sec	Marie-José Perec France	48.83 sec
Juliet Cuthbert Jamaica	22.02 sec	Olga Bryzgina Unified Team	49.05 sec
Merlene Ottey Jamaica	22.09 sec	Ximena Restrepo Gaviria Colombia	49.64 sec

The picture below shows the end of one of these two races.

15. Is this a picture of the 200-meter or the 400-meter sprint? Explain your reasoning.

16. What do you think the winning times in the women's 100-meter race were? Explain your reasoning.

15. 200-meter race

Looking at the picture, students may be able to see that the distance between the first-place runner and the second-place runner is about three times the distance between the second-place runner and the third-place runner.

Looking at the times listed in the problem, they may see that in the 400-meter race the time difference between Bryzgina and Restrepo Gaviria (0.59 sec) is much greater than that between Perec and Bryzgina (0.22 sec), which does not correspond to the picture. So, students may guess that the picture shows the finish of the 200-meter race.

16. Answers will vary. Accept any times around 10 seconds. Explanations will also vary.

Possible explanation:

Since the winning times for the 200-meter race are between 21 and 23 seconds, the winning times for the 100-meter race would be between 10 and 13 seconds.

Overview Students match a picture of the finish of a track race with the runners' times.

About the Mathematics The problems on this page involve decimal numbers that represent units of time. Units of time cannot be changed by simply moving the decimal point in the number to the right or left as students did when dealing with metric units. You may need to remind students that there are 60, not 100, seconds in a minute. It may be easier for students to compute with the decimal numbers as they appear in the problems without changing the measurement units to hundredths of a second, for example.

Planning Students can work on these problems individually or in pairs.

Comments about the Problems

15. Informal Assessment This problem assesses students' understanding of place value and its use in ordering decimals and their ability to choose an appropriate visual model or strategy to represent and solve problems involving decimals.

To solve this problem, students must understand that, in both races, the difference between the first and second runners' times should be compared to the difference between the second and third runners' times. Students should also understand how the value of a digit in a decimal number is related to its position.

16. Informal Assessment This problem assesses students' ability to estimate and compute with decimals and to choose an appropriate visual model or strategy to represent and solve problems involving decimals. It also assesses their understanding of place value and its use in ordering decimals.

Extension You may ask students to solve the following problem as an extension to problem **16:**

The winning times in the women's 100-meter race at the 1992 Olympics were as follows:

Gold: 10.82 sec
Silver: 10.83 sec
Bronze:10.84 sec

By how much do these times differ? [by 0.01 seconds or one one-hundredth of a second].

Cycle Racing

Cycle races are generally timed races over a given distance or distance races during a length of time.

Below are some world cycling records.

1 kilometer = 1,000 meters

1 kilometer is about a 9- to 12-minute walk.

Racer	Kilometers (in one hour)	Dates
Ritter	48.65392	Oct. 10, 1968
Merckx	49.431957	Oct. 25, 1972
Moser	50.808423	Jan. 19, 1984
Moser	51.151350	Jan. 23, 1984

17. a. How many meters did Ritter cycle in one hour?

b. If it takes about 9 to 12 minutes to walk 1 kilometer, about how long would it take to walk the distance Ritter cycled in one hour?

18. By how many kilometers per hour did Moser break his own record on January 23, 1984? Explain your calculation.

19. By how many kilometers per hour did the record increase from 1968 to 1984?

17. a. 48.65392 kilometers = 48653.92 meters

b. Answers will vary. If students walk one kilometer in about 12 minutes then they can walk approximately five kilometers in one hour. Walking forty-nine kilometers would take almost 10 hours. Students may estimate more than 10 hours to include rest stops.

18. 0.342927 kilometer per hour

19. 2.49743 kilometers per hour

Overview Students use and interpret decimals that represent cycling distances measured in kilometers.

Planning Students may work in pairs or in small groups on problems **17–19.** Discuss the different strategies that students use to solve each problem.

Comments about the Problems

17. If students are having difficulty, you may suggest the following strategy (assuming they know that one kilometer is equal to 1,000 meters): First have students estimate the number of kilometers that Ritter cycled in one hour [about 48 kilometers]. Then ask students to convert this distance into meters [48 kilometers = about 48,000 meters]. Students can use this estimate to position the decimal point in the correct place in the answer.

18. Encourage students to explain their calculations. Their explanations need not include the traditional algorithmic procedure. For example, students may notice that the distance is less than one kilometer. They may then change the distance in kilometers to a distance in centimeters or round each number before calculating their answers.

19. This question is similar to problem **18.** Be sure students realize that they need to use the speed record set on January 23, 1984, when determining the increase. Encourage students to use methods that involve mental and/or written computations rather than calculators. To encourage them to reason out their answers, you may want to ask students questions such as: *Was the increase greater than or less than one kilometer?* [greater than one kilometer]

Did You Know? Students may wonder how it is possible to measure a cyclist's speed so precisely. It helps to know how a race is organized. A single cyclist rides on a track of known length for one hour. The number of laps is recorded. When the hour is over, each cyclist finishes the last lap and his or her final time is recorded to one one-hundredth of a second. Because the number of laps and the length of a single lap are known, the total distance can be calculated. Then the final distance is divided by the final time to find each cyclist's speed in kilometers per hour.

Summary

Decimal numbers can be interpreted in various ways. For example:

$$3.751 \text{ meters} =$$

3 meters + 7 decimeters + 5 centimeters + 1 millimeter

or

$$3 + \frac{7}{10} + \frac{5}{100} + \frac{1}{1000} \text{ meters}$$

or

3,751 millimeters

or

$$\frac{3751}{1000} \text{ meters}$$

The decimal system allows for unlimited precision. Every digit you add to the right of the decimal point represents a unit 10 times smaller than the last unit. For example:

$$0.000007 \quad = \quad \frac{7}{1,000,000}$$

$$0.0000078 \quad = \quad \frac{7}{1,000,000} \quad + \quad \frac{8}{10,000,000} \quad or \quad \frac{78}{10,000,000}$$

Summary Question

20. Find at least three newspaper clippings that contain decimals. For each clipping, write questions (and answers) about the decimals that are used.

20. Answers will vary. Student questions and answers will reflect their understanding and use of decimals in real-world situations.

Extension 1

1. a. ΩΩΩ – – – – – – – – JJJJJ ς

b. Ω J J ςςς

c. ςςςς

d. ΩΩJ J J

Extension 2

2. The discussion should include the following points:

In our decimal system, numerals have meaning depending on where they appear in relation to the decimal point. The decimal system also uses zeros as placeholders.

Decimal	Cleopatra & Daughters
value dependent on position of digit in relation to decimal point	value determined by character alone
zero used as placeholder	no use of zero as placeholder
digit can change to show multiples of a given value	characters repeated to show multiples of a given value

Materials local newspapers, especially the sports sections (about six copies per class)

Overview Students read the Summary, which describes the relationships between decimals and the metric system. Students write and answer questions about decimals that they find in newspaper articles.

Planning You may have students work on problem **20** as homework and/or an assessment. You can also use the Extension below to evaluate students' understanding of our decimal number system. After students complete Section C, you may assign appropriate activities from the Try This! section, located on pages 37–40 of the Student Book, as homework.

Comments about the Problems

20. Informal Assessment This problem assesses students' ability to use decimals in a context, such as money or measurement, and to represent and use decimals in a variety of equivalent forms to solve problems in real-world and mathematical situations. It also assesses their understanding of the metric system and its relationship to decimals, their understanding of decimals as they relate to refinement in the measurement process, and their understanding of place value and its use in ordering decimals.

Writing Opportunity You might want to ask students to write their questions and answers to problem **20** in their journals.

Extension You can use the following problems to make a connection with the previous section. Students' answers will provide evidence of their understanding of the decimal number system.

1. How would you write the following numbers in the notation used by Cleopatra & Daughters in Section A?

   a. 3.751
   b. 1.023
   c. 0.004
   d. 2.030

2. Write a paragraph comparing our decimal number system to the Cleopatra & Daughters' number system. (Possible answers are provided in the Solutions column.)

Work Students Do

Students compare and order decimals in a variety of contexts. They read about a fictional television game show called *The Price Is Slime* and compare and order decimals to see how close various price guesses are to the actual prices of items. They then use a number line strategy to determine which guess is closest to a given price. Next, students estimate the total cost of grocery items and decide which of the items can be bought with a given amount of money. Students round large numbers (population figures over one million) and determine how precise distance measurements for hiking and biking trails should be.

Goals

Students will:

- use decimals in a context, such as money or measurement;*
- estimate and compute with decimals;
- understand place value and its use in ordering decimals;
- understand the metric system and its relationship to decimals;
- understand decimals as they relate to refinement in the measurement process;
- represent and use decimals in a variety of equivalent forms to solve problems in real-world and mathematical situations;*
- choose an appropriate visual model or strategy to represent and solve problems involving decimals.

These goals are assessed in other sections of this unit.

Pacing

- approximately five or six 45-minute class sessions

Vocabulary

- liter
- milliliter
- rounding
- significant digits

About the Mathematics

In this section, three strategies are used to compare and order decimals. The first strategy involves using a number line model, which visually aids students in ordering decimals. The second strategy, one used in previous sections, is that of converting the units. For example, in this section, dollars are converted to pennies, kilometers are converted to meters, and whole-number populations are rounded to millions. The third strategy is that of transferring decimals to a more familiar context. For example, if students are having difficulty dealing with decimals within the context of distances on trails in a national park, they may transfer the decimals to a context they understand, such as money.

At times, comparing and ordering decimals are relatively simple tasks, such as when ordering the scores 3.2, 4.6, and 2.0. At other times, these tasks can be more challenging, such as when finding a score that is halfway between 8.5 and 8.6.

Decimals, such as 6.784, can be rounded to one decimal place by determining if 6.784 is closer to 6.7 or 6.8. Students can place the number 6.784 on a number line between 6.7 and 6.8 to determine that 6.784 is closer to 6.8 than 6.7.

Materials

- Student Activity Sheets 3–5, pages 97–99 of the Teacher Guide (one of each per student)
- small purchased items (such as erasers, pencils, or candy), page 61 of the Teacher Guide, optional (10 different items per class)
- transparencies of newspaper advertisements, page 61 of the Teacher Guide, optional (one or two per class)
- overhead projector, page 61 of the Teacher Guide, optional (one per class)
- newspaper advertisements, page 67 of the Teacher Guide, optional (several ads per group of students)
- atlas or almanac showing the local population of your city, page 73 of the Teacher Guide (one per group of students)
- meter sticks, metric tape measures, or trundle wheels, page 77 of the Teacher Guide, optional (one per pair of students)
- one- or two-liter container, page 81 of the Teacher Guide, optional (one per class)

Planning Instruction

Make sure students understand that decimals, fractions, and money can all be used to represent the same quantity. If students do not grasp this concept, they may have difficulty comparing and ordering decimals. They will gain further insight into this concept through the remaining situations in this section.

This section uses the metric system in several contexts. You may want to show a one- and/or two-liter container to students who are unfamiliar with liters.

Students may work in pairs or in small groups on all of the problems in this section.

There are no optional problems. Be sure to discuss students' solutions and strategies for problems 1–8, 12, 14, 15, and 19–25 with the whole class.

Homework

- Problems 2–4 (pages 62 and 64 of the Teacher Guide) can be assigned as homework. The Extensions (pages 61, 67, 75, and 77 of the Teacher Guide) can also be assigned as homework. After students complete Section D, you may assign appropriate activities from the Try This! section, located on pages 37–40 of the *Measure for Measure* Student Book. The Try This! activities reinforce the key math concepts introduced in this section.

Planning Assessment

- Problems 2 and 3 can be used to informally assess students' understanding of place value and its use in ordering decimals.
- The Extension on page 67 of the Teacher Guide can be used to informally assess students' ability to estimate and compute with decimals.
- Problems 22, 23, and 34 can be used to informally assess students' understanding of decimals as they relate to refinement in the measurement process.
- Problem 29 can be used to informally assess students' understanding of the metric system and its relationship to decimals, and their ability to choose an appropriate visual model or strategy to represent and solve problems involving decimals.
- Problem 32 can be used to informally assess students' understanding of place value and its use in ordering decimals and their understanding of the metric system and its relationship to decimals.

D. ORDERING DECIMALS

Guess the Price

On the new television game show *The Price Is Slime,* contestants try to guess the prices of various items. The goal of the game is to get as close to the right price as possible, either over or under. The person whose guess is farthest from the real price has green slime dropped on his or her head from above.

John, Neysa, Amy, and Lemar are the contestants in today's show. Their first task is to guess the price of *The Price Is Slime* home game.

Guesses:

John: $8.50   Amy: $7.50
Neysa: $7.75   Lemar: $8.00

The actual price is $7.95.

Materials small purchased items (such as erasers, pencils, or candy), optional (10 different items per class); transparencies of newspaper advertisements, optional (one or two per class); overhead projector, optional (one per class)

Overview Students are introduced to a fictional television game show, *The Price Is Slime.* Within this context students order and compare decimals to determine which amount is closest to and which amount is farthest away from the given price. There are no problems on this page. Problems involving this game begin on page 26 of the Student Book.

About the Mathematics The context of money will help to further develop students' understanding of decimal place value and of comparing and ordering decimals. Students may relate decimals to money amounts when working with decimals in other contexts within this section.

Planning You may want to start with a short class discussion about the television game show. If you decide to do the Extension suggested below, have several small items on hand.

Extension Students may enjoy playing a variation of *The Price Is Slime* game that will provide more practice with comparing decimals. Purchase small items familiar to students, such as candy, erasers, and pencils. Hold up one item at a time. Have students guess the price of that item. Then reveal the item's actual retail price. Have students determine who came closest to the actual price and award that item to the student.

Another possibility is to have students guess the prices of items shown in newspaper ads. You can make transparencies of the ads and show the items on the overhead projector. Be sure to cover the prices in the ads before making the transparencies.

$8.00
LEMAR'S ANSWER

$7.95
ACTUAL PRICE

$7.75
NEYSA'S ANSWER

The host says that Lemar's is the best answer, but Neysa disagrees. She argues that her answer is closest because it sounds the best: "Seven seventy-five sounds almost the same as seven ninety-five. Eight dollars sounds completely different!" Lemar claims that eight dollars differs just a little bit from $7.95.

Amy exclaims, "I know how you can see it!" She draws a number line, explaining, "Here is $8.00; here is $7.95; and here is $7.75."

1. a. Whose guess is closest to the actual price?

b. Who gets slimed?

c. Use a number line to show your answers.

The next task is to guess the price of a videocassette.

Guesses:

John: $13.55   Amy: $13.50

Neysa: $14.00   Lemar: $13.80

The actual price is $13.65.

2. a. Show these guesses on a number line.

b. Whose guess is closest to the actual price?

c. Who gets slimed?

The last task is to guess the price of a pair of jogging shoes.

Guesses:

John: $84.95   Amy: $85.00

Neysa: $88.80   Lemar: $86.75

The actual price is $87.75.

3. a. Show these guesses on a number line.

b. Whose guess is closest to the actual price?

c. Who gets slimed?

Solutions and Samples
of student work

1. a. Lemar's guess is closest to the actual price.

b. John gets slimed because his guess farthest from the actual price.

c.

2. a.

b. John's guess is closest to the actual price.

c. Neysa gets slimed because her guess is farthest from the actual price.

3. a.

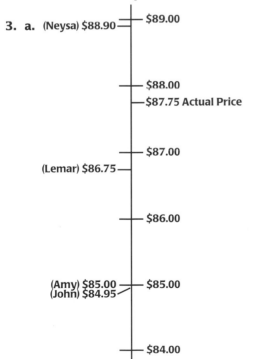

b. Lemar's guess is closest to the actual price.

c. John gets slimed because his guess is farthest from the actual price.

Overview Students compare various guesses of the prices of several items. They use a number line to determine which guess is closest to the actual price for each item.

About the Mathematics The number line is used here as a model with which to compare and order decimals. Using this visual model, students can immediately see the position of each decimal number on the number line. Often, looking at the decimals alone can be confusing. For example, in problem **1** some students may incorrectly reason, *I see a 7 in 7.75, and a number with a 7 in it will be closer to 7.95 than a number with an 8 in it.* The number line can help illustrate the error in this reasoning.

Planning If you did the Extension on the previous page, you can have students solve problem **1,** discuss this problem, and then use problems **2** and **3** as assessments and/or homework.

Comments about the Problems

1–3. In these problems, students become aware of the relative value of decimals. Discuss students' strategies for at least one of these problems.

2–3. Informal Assessment These problems assess students' understanding of place value and its use in ordering decimals. They may also be assigned as homework.

The Supermarket

juice
$0.66
per bottle

peanut butter
$1.82

bread
$1.24

chips
$0.69

George had to pick up a few items at the supermarket. The prices shown include tax.

At the checkout, George worried that he did not have enough money. He emptied his pockets and found the amount pictured below.

4. Did George have enough money to pay for all of his purchases? Explain.

5. If he had enough, what else could he have bought? If he did not have enough, what item should he have left behind?

6. Estimate the total amount for each column below. Be prepared to defend your answers.

a.	**b.**	**c.**	**d.**
$1.25	$2.98	$3.25	$0.80
$1.25	$1.95	$4.75	$1.25
$1.25	$0.97	$2.01	$1.99
$1.25		$4.05	$1.19

4. If the items cost about $6.00, and George had about $5.00 in his pocket, he did not have enough money to pay for the items.

Explanations will vary. One possible explanation:

To compute the cost of the items, I estimated that three times the price of one bottle of juice ($0.66) is around $2.00, and the price of the peanut butter ($1.82) is almost $2.00. The last two items together are also about $2.00. So George needed a total of about $6.00. In George's pocket, there were four dollar bills, three quarters, and several dimes. George only had about $5.00.

5. Answers will vary. To determine what item George should have left behind, students must calculate the exact total cost as if he had bought everything. The total is $5.73. There was only $5.30 in George's pocket. So he should have left behind an item that costs at least 43 cents.

Some students may argue that George should have left behind the article that he needed the least. Others may argue that he should have left one of the drinks behind because he took three bottles of juice.

6. Estimates may vary. Possible estimates:

  a. $5.00

  b. about $6.00

  c. about $14.00

  d. about $5.00

Overview Students estimate the total cost of grocery items and decide which items can be purchased with a given amount of money.

About the Mathematics The strategy of changing the measurement units can be used in this context. Converting each dollar amount to cents may help students more easily estimate the totals. These problems demonstrate that the number of coins (for example, pennies) does not always make a big difference in the total amount of money.

Planning Students can work on problems **4–6** in pairs or in small groups. Discuss students' solutions and strategies. Problem **4** can be assigned as homework.

Comments about the Problems

4. **Homework** This problem can be assigned as homework. To solve it, students must first count George's money and then estimate the total price of the groceries to determine whether or not he has enough money to pay for them. Remind students to round the grocery item prices up (unless the price is only slightly above one dollar). Encourage students to discuss how they counted the money.

5. To calculate the exact total cost of the items, students can convert the dollar amount of each item to cents and then calculate the total cost (3 × 66 cents) + 182 cents + 124 cents + 69 cents = 573 cents. They can then convert the total cost back to dollars ($5.73).

The price of the item left behind may not be obvious to all students. To solve this problem, students may convert the dollar amounts into cents again and calculate the difference between 573 cents and 530 cents.

6. Have students explain how they got their answers. Discuss when it is appropriate to estimate and when it is just as easy to calculate an exact answer. For example, the total amount in problem **6a** can easily be calculated if you know that four quarters equal one dollar. Likewise, the total amount in **6c** can easily be calculated if you know that one quarter and 75 cents make one dollar.

At the local supermarket, items are priced as follows:

one box of tissues: $1.22

one pint of yogurt: $0.75

one pound of bananas: $0.39

one gallon of milk: $2.05

7. Find the cost of the following purchases:

   a. one pint of yogurt and one pound of bananas

   b. one gallon of milk and two boxes of tissues

   c. four boxes of tissues

   d. four pints of yogurt, three pounds of bananas, and eight gallons of milk

8. a. Suppose your grocery bill comes to $10.35, but you have only $10.00. You decide to put back one gallon of milk. What is your total now?

   b. If your total grocery bill is $8.69 and you pay with $10.00, how much will you get back in change?

When comparing numbers, you may find it helpful to use a number line. It can also help to think of numbers that have two places after the decimal point in terms of dollars and cents.

It is important to have a few "reference points" when estimating. For example:

whole numbers	0.00
(3.10 is a little more than 3.00;	
6.93 is a little less than 7.00)	
halves	0.50
(0.43 is about 0.50;	
12.61 is about 12.50)	
quarters	0.25
(0.23 is about 0.25)	
(0.80 is about 0.75)	0.75

You encounter decimals every day. Some have one place after the decimal point (for example, figure-skating scores at the Olympics); others have two places after the decimal point (for example, prices at the grocery store). In the next lesson, you will take a closer look at numbers with one place after the decimal point.

7. a. $1.14 ($0.75 + $0.39)

   b. $4.49 ($2.05 + $2.44)

   c. $4.88 ($1.22 × 4)

   d. $20.57

      ((4 × $0.75) + (3 × $0.39) + (8 × $2.05))

8. a. $8.30 ($10.35 − $2.05)

    Strategies to calculate $10.35 − $2.05:

    $10.35 − $2.00 − $0.05 =

    $8.35 − $0.05 = $8.30

    or

    $10.35 − $0.05 − $2.00 =

    $10.30 − $2.00 = $8.30

   b. $1.31 ($10.00 − $8.69)

    Strategy to calculate $10.00 − $8.69:

    $10.00 − $8.69 =

    $10.00 − $8.70 + $0.01 =

    $1.30 + $0.01 = $1.31

Materials newspaper advertisements, optional (several ads per group of students)

Overview Students compute with decimals to find the total cost of purchasing different grocery items. Number lines and money "reference points" (wholes, halves, and quarters) are suggested as aids with which to compare and estimate decimal amounts.

Planning Students may work in pairs or in small groups on problems **7** and **8**.After students work on problems **7** and **8**, discuss these problems with the whole class, making connections to the money reference points. You can use the Extension below as an assessment. Be aware that this Extension requires some advance preparation.

Comments about the Problems

  7. Challenge students to use their number sense to answer these questions. For example, some students may compute the cost of four pints of yogurt using repeated addition: $0.75 + $0.75 + $0.75 + $0.75. Other students may see that $0.75 + $0.75 = $1.50 and then double that amount to find the total cost.

  8. Discuss students' strategies. Some students may convert the dollar amounts to cents and then compute to find their answers. See the Solutions column for examples of various students' strategies.

Extension This activity can be used to assess students' ability to estimate and compute with decimals.

Give groups of students several newspaper advertisements. Specify an amount of money with which students can buy advertised items. Ask them estimate what items they can buy.

Students' answers may give you insight into the strategies and concepts they have developed thus far:
- calculating with rounded numbers (for example, 1.98 rounded to 2.00),
- calculating with familiar decimals (for example, 0.25), and
- understanding decimal place value.

Talent Search

Amateur singers sometimes dream of becoming big stars. The Dream Town USA talent search is organized every year to give such singers a chance to win a recording contract. Sixteen young, talented singers are invited to compete in the first round.

The singers are scored by a panel of judges. After the first round, the top eight singers go on to the semifinals. The top four in the semifinal round then go to the final round. After the final round, one singer is chosen for the recording contract.

In the table below, you see the names of this year's singers and their scores from the first round.

Singer	Score
Eileen	7.0
Gilberto	6.5
John	7.3
Kenesha	8.7
Janice	6.8
Fernando	7.6
James	7.1
Chen	8.3

Singer	Score
Grace	7.8
Kate	7.6
Yolanda	6.5
Vivian	7.0
Robert	8.1
Verzell	7.7
Alicia	6.7
Miwa	7.9

9. Which singers went on to the semifinals?

9. Kenesha, Chen, Robert, Fernando, Grace, Kate, Verzell, and Miwa went on to the semifinals.

Overview Within the context of a talent search, students compare and order decimal numbers representing scores in a singing contest. The decimal numbers, such as 7.8, are made up of a whole number and one decimal.

About the Mathematics The context of the talent search (on pages 29 and 30 of the Student Book) is the first time in which students work explicitly with three-digit decimals, as they do in problem **15.**

If students are having difficulty determining a decimal number that is halfway between two given decimal numbers (for example, 5.5 and 5.6), encourage them to place a zero after the last digit in each number (5.50 and 5.60). Have them then convert these decimal numbers to cents (550 and 560) to find the number halfway between them. You may also have students refer to the number system developed by Cleopatra and Daughters in Section A or suggest that they draw a number line. Also see the Hints & Comments on page 71.

Planning Students may work in pairs or in small groups on problem **9.** Briefly discuss students' strategies, if time permits.

Comments about the Problems

9. Encourage students to explain how they figured out which contestants went on to the semifinals. Some may have seen immediately that Kenesha, Chen, and Robert were chosen, because their scores are the only ones above eight points.

The score box below shows the results of the semifinals.

Singer	Score
Chen	8.2
Kate	7.9
Verzell	8.0
Miwa	8.7
Fernando	8.6
Kenesha	8.3
Robert	
Grace	

10. Order these results on a number line.

11. Robert was the seventh person to sing in the semifinals. The judges gave him a score that was halfway between Fernando's and Miwa's. What was Robert's score?

12. Grace was the last singer. The judges gave her a score that was just a little bit better than Kenesha's. What could Grace's score have been?

13. Which four singers went on to the finals?

At the finals, the judges were very impressed with the contestants. Almost all of the scores were above nine. Grace was the first to sing in the finals, and the judges gave her a score of 9.9. Fernando was next. The judges thought he was just a little better than Grace. However, they did not want to give him a 10.

14. What score do you think the judges gave Fernando?

15. The judges thought Robert's score should be exactly halfway between the scores of Grace and Fernando. What score did Robert get?

16. Miwa's score was 8.9. List the four finalists and their scores in order. Who won the competition?

10.

7.9 8.0   8.2 8.3   8.6 8.7

11. Robert's score was 8.65.

12. Answers will vary. A possible range is between 8.31 and 8.4.

13. Miwa, Robert, Fernando, and Grace went on to the finals.

14. Answers will vary. Accept scores within the range of 9.91 to 9.99.

15. Answers will vary depending on students' answers to problem **14.** For example, if a student answered 9.91 for problem **14,** he or she should give an answer of 9.905 for problem **15.** If the student answered 9.95 for problem **14,** he or she should give an answer of 9.925.

16. The scores will vary (see problems **14** and **15**). However, the order of the four finalists was:

First place: Fernando
Second place: Robert
Third place: Grace
Fourth place: Miwa

Overview Students continue to order and compare the decimal scores of contestants using a number line.

About the Mathematics In problem **11,** if you consider only the digits in the tenth's place of the numbers 8.6 and 8.7, it is difficult to find a number that lies exactly between them. One strategy is to convert the decimal numbers to monetary amounts ($8.60 and $8.70) and compare the two decimal digits in both numbers. Most students will now be able to determine that 8.65 is exactly halfway between $8.60 and $8.70. This strategy can also be used to determine what number is exactly halfway between numbers with two decimal places, such as 9.55 and 9.60. Since 9.55 is the same as 9.550 and 9.60 is the same as 9.600, then 9.575 would fall exactly between 9.55 and 9.60. It is also possible to relate these decimals to the context of measurement (using millimeters as thousandths of a meter).

Planning Students can work on problems **10–16** in pairs or in small groups. Be sure to discuss problems **12, 14,** and **15.**

Comments about the Problems

10. Students may draw a horizontal or vertical number line. Check to see that the numbers are ordered correctly.

11. If students are having difficulty with this problem, suggest that they use one of the strategies suggested in the About the Mathematics section above.

12. Students may find it helpful to draw a number line.

13. This problem can also be solved without knowing the exact scores of Robert's and Grace (see problems **11** and **12**). If the known scores of the six contestants are placed on a number line and Robert and Grace's scores are estimated and placed on the number line, it is possible to decide which four singers will go on to the finals.

14. You may remind students of the number system developed by Cleopatra and Daughters in Section A.

15. Some students may find it easier to figure out what number is halfway between 9,900 (Grace's score) and 9,910 (a possible score for Fernando).

Big Cities in the United States

Below is a list of cities for which the population of the metropolitan area was over a million people in 1990.

City	Population
Atlanta	2,959,950
Baltimore	2,382,172
Boston	5,455,403
Buffalo	1,189,288
Chicago	8,239,820
Cincinnati	1,817,571
Cleveland	2,859,644
Dallas	4,037,282
Denver	1,980,140
Detroit	5,187,171
Houston	3,731,131
Indianapolis	1,380,491
Kansas City, MO	1,582,875
Los Angeles	14,531,529

City	Population
Miami	3,192,582
Milwaukee	1,607,183
New Orleans	1,285,270
New York City	19,549,649
Orlando	1,224,852
Philadelphia	5,892,937
Pittsburgh	2,394,811
Portland, OR	1,793,476
St. Louis, MO	2,492,525
San Antonio	1,324,749
San Diego	2,498,016
San Francisco	6,253,311
Seattle	2,970,328
Washington, D.C.	4,223,485

17. Does it make sense to report the 1990 population of Cincinnati as exactly 1,817,571? Why or why not?

18. What is the current population of the city in which you live?

19. Compare the current population of your city with the 1990 population listed for San Antonio.

20. Compare the current population of your city with the 1990 population listed for New York City.

Solutions and Samples
of student work

17. It does not make sense to report Cincinnati as having a population of exactly 1,817,571. Because populations are constantly changing, it is impossible to give an exact number.

18. Answers will vary depending on the population of the city in which students live.

19. Answers will vary. Possible answers:

    Suppose students live in a city with a population of 1,255 people. They might round this number to 1,250 and round San Antonio's population to 1,000,000. Students may then note that San Antonio is 800 times larger than their city. Other students may say that their city is smaller than San Antonio or that it has 998,750 fewer people.

20. Answers may vary. Possible answer:

    Suppose, again, that students live in a city with a population of 1,255 people. From problem **19**, they know that a city of 1 million people, such as San Antonio, is 800 times larger than their own city. Because New York City is about 19 times larger than San Antonio, New York would be about 15,200 times larger than the students' city.

Hints and Comments

Materials atlas or almanac showing the population of your city (one per group of students)

Overview Students compare the populations of U.S. cities that have over one million people.

About the Mathematics When comparing large numbers, all digits are not always significant. Therefore, large numbers are often rounded and expressed in other units before being compared. For example, the number 7,159,084 can be rounded to 7,000,000 and expressed as 7 million or 7.2 million. This strategy is introduced on the page 31 of the Student Book to make a connection to the main concepts of this unit: decimals and the refinement of units.

Planning You might want to start with a short class discussion to introduce the context of the populations of large metropolitan areas. Some students may not be able to distinguish between the terms *city, town, suburb, village,* and *metropolitan area.* A discussion of how they apply to the students' environment may help.

Be sure to have several copies of an atlas or almanac on hand for information about your local population. Students can work in pairs or in small groups on problems **17–20.** Discuss students' solutions and strategies for problems **19** and **20.**

Comments about the Problems

17–20. The purpose of these questions is to give students a sense of the size of 1,000,000 or more.

19. Discuss students' answers. Encourage them to talk about the information that each answer gives. Also have them discuss why one answer may be more appropriate than another.

City	Population	Population (to the nearest million)
Atlanta	2,959,950	3
Baltimore	2,382,172	
Boston	5,455,403	
Buffalo	1,189,288	
Chicago	8,239,820	
Cincinnati	1,817,571	
Cleveland	2,859,644	
Dallas	4,037,282	
Denver	1,980,140	
Detroit	5,187,171	
Houston	3,731,131	
Indianapolis	1,380,491	1
Kansas City, MO	1,582,875	
Los Angeles	14,531,529	
Miami	3,192,582	
Milwaukee	1,607,183	
New Orleans	1,285,270	
New York City	19,549,649	
Orlando	1,224,852	
Philadelphia	5,892,937	
Pittsburgh	2,394,811	
Portland, OR	1,793,476	
St. Louis, MO	2,492,525	
San Antonio	1,324,749	
San Diego	2,498,016	
San Francisco	6,253,311	
Seattle	2,970,328	
Washington, D.C.	4,223,485	

The editor of a local newspaper wants to print a table showing the 10 largest metropolitan areas of the United States. She decides the best way to do this is to round the population of each city to the nearest million. For example, the population of Atlanta—2,959,950—can be rounded to 3 million.

21. Use **Student Activity Sheet 3** to round each population to the nearest million. Atlanta and Indianapolis have been done for you.

Newspapers often express the population of a city as a decimal. For example, the population of New York City—19,549,649—can be written as 19.5 million.

22. Compare the populations of New Orleans and Orlando. How many decimal places would the editor need to use if she wanted to show that New Orleans has the larger population?

23. Now the editor wants to make a list of the 12 largest metropolitan areas. What is the fewest number of digits she must compare to do this?

You can write the populations of cities in several different ways. For example, the population of Pittsburgh can be written as:

2 million
2.4 million
2.39 million
2.395 million

24. Explain how you might get these numbers from the population of the Pittsburgh metropolitan area given in the table.

21.

City	Population	Population (to the nearest million)
Atlanta	2,959,950	3
Baltimore	2,382,172	2
Boston	5,455,403	5
Buffalo	1,189,288	1
Chicago	8,239,820	8
Cincinnati	1,817,571	2
Cleveland	2,859,644	3
Dallas	4,037,282	4
Denver	1,980,140	2
Detroit	5,187,171	5
Houston	3,731,131	4
Indianapolis	1,380,491	1
Kansas City, MO	1,582,875	2
Los Angeles	14,531,529	15
Miami	3,192,582	3
Milwaukee	1,607,183	2
New Orleans	1,285,270	1
New York City	19,549,649	20
Orlando	1,224,852	1
Philadelphia	5,892,937	6
Pittsburgh	2,394,811	2
Portland, OR	1,793,476	2
St. Louis, MO	2,492,525	2
San Antonio	1,324,749	1
San Diego	2,498,016	2
San Francisco	6,253,311	6
Seattle	2,970,328	3
Washington, D.C.	4,223,485	4

22. The editor would need to use two decimal places to show that New Orleans's population is larger:

New Orleans: 1.28 million
Orlando: 1.22 million

23. The editor needs to use two decimal places to show that Seattle (2.97 million) is the 12th largest city, not Atlanta (2.95 million).

24. 2,394,811 rounded to the nearest million is 2 million.

2,394,811 rounded to the nearest tenth of a million is 2.4 million.

2,394,811 rounded to the nearest hundredth of a million is 2.39 million.

2,394,811 rounded to the nearest thousandth of a million is 2.395 million.

Materials Student Activity Sheet 3 (one per student)

Overview Students round population figures to the nearest million.

Planning Students may work in pairs or in small groups on these problems. Depending on students' experiences with large numbers and place value, you may decide to start with the Extension. This activity will help students in solving problems **22** and **23.** You may also use problems **22** and **23** as assessments. Be sure to discuss students' solutions and strategies for problems **21–24.**

Comments about the Problems

21. Students should have an understanding of how to round numbers without explicitly studying rounding rules. After students have looked at the population figures, ask them to round the population of Los Angeles (14,531,529) to the nearest million. Most students will be able to correctly round this number to 15 million. Some students may have difficulty rounding population figures of cities like Boston (5,455,403). In this case, Boston's population is closer to 5 million than to 6 million.

22–23. Informal Assessment These problems assess students' understanding of decimals as they relate to refinement in measurement.

Extension Ask students to explain the strategies they would use to compare and order the population figures of these cities. They may come up with useful suggestions. Then have students participate in the following activity:

Ask students to cover all but the millions digit of each number in the population column with a piece of paper. They will then immediately see that New York City has the largest population, since this city has the only population figure of at least 19 million. Students will then easily find the city with the second-largest population, since Los Angeles is the only city with a population of at least 14 million. Most students will be able to identify Chicago and San Francisco as the cities with the third- and fourth-largest populations using the same reasoning.

The Great Outdoors

Trails from Bear Valley	Distances (one way)
Arch Rock	6,601 m
Coast Camp	9,338 m
Divide Meadow	2,576 m
Glen Camp	7,406 m
Palomarin	18,998 m
Sky Camp	4,347 m
Wildcat Camp	10,143 m
From Fivebrooks	**(one way)**
Wildcat Camp	10,787 m

Source: National Park Service, Point Reyes National Seashore.

Point Reyes National Seashore is a national park in California. This park has several hiking and biking trails.

Alice is a park ranger at Point Reyes. She needs to know the lengths of the trails in order to make a brochure. She walks each path pushing a trundle wheel that is connected to an odometer, a device for measuring distances.

Alice makes a table like the one on the left. Alice's friends think that the distances should not be given in meters because the measurement is too precise.

25. Do you agree with Alice's friends? Why or why not?

25. Answers will vary. Possible response:

Yes. I agree with Alice's friends. Because 1 kilometer equals 1,000 meters and all the distances in the table are more than 1,000 meters, it would make sense to show the distances in kilometers. However, this might mean that the distances will be decimal numbers.

Materials meter sticks, metric tape measures, or trundle wheels, optional (one per pair of students)

Overview Students examine a table that lists the distances (in meters) of biking and hiking trails at a national park. Students determine whether or not the measurement unit of a meter makes sense for the given distances.

About the Mathematics Changing the context to distances in meters will help to reinforce students' understanding of decimals, changing units, and the need for refinement in measurement. Problems **25–31** are similar to those on pages 31 and 32 of the Student Book.

Planning You may begin with a short discussion of what a trundle wheel is and how it works. If your school has a trundle wheel, show it to the class. Students can work in pairs or in small groups on problem **25.** Discuss this problem with the whole class.

Comments about the Problems

25. Students should focus on the purpose of providing the distances listed in the table rather than on whether or not Alice measured the distances correctly.

Extension To give students a sense of the length of one meter and how distances are measured in meters, have them measure the distance around the perimeter of the school grounds or the length of the hallway outside the classroom in meters. They can use either a meter stick, a metric measuring tape, or a trundle wheel. This activity prepares students for the problems on the following page.

26. Describe a distance of 1 kilometer in your neighborhood.

27. Look at the table on **Student Activity Sheet 4.** Round each distance to the nearest kilometer.

> **1,000 meters = 1 kilometer**
> A large pace is about 1 meter.
> If you walk 1,000 paces,
> you walk 1 kilometer.

Alice changes her measurement to kilometers, but decides that they are not accurate enough. She decides to give the distances in tenths of kilometers. For example, the distance from Bear Valley to Arch Rock is 6.6 kilometers.

28. Complete the table on **Student Activity Sheet 4.** Round each distance to the nearest tenth of a kilometer. Explain how you got your answers.

The odometer on Jeffrey's bike indicates distances in tenths of kilometers. When he rides the bike trail from Bear Valley to Arch Rock and back, Jeffrey's odometer registers 13.1 kilometers.

29. Is Jeffrey's odometer wrong? (Hint: Look at **Student Activity Sheet 4** and calculate the round-trip in meters.)

Jeffrey tries to improve his speed with every trip he makes. The table below shows his average speeds from last week.

Sunday	20.3 km/h
Monday	20.7 km/h
Tuesday	21.4 km/h
Wednesday	21.1 km/h
Thursday	20.8 km/h
Friday	21.6 km/h
Saturday	21.2 km/h

30. Did Jeffrey improve his speed? Explain.

31. What is the difference between his lowest and highest average speeds?

26. Answers will vary. Note that most people can walk about one kilometer in 12 minutes.

27. One-way trail distances:

From Bear Valley

Arch Rock	7 km
Coast Camp	9 km
Divide Meadow	3 km
Glen Camp	7 km
Palomarin	19 km
Sky Camp	4 km
Wildcat Camp	10 km

From Fivebrooks

Wildcat Camp	11 km

28. One-way trail distances:

From Bear Valley

Arch Rock	6.6 km
Coast Camp	9.3 km
Divide Meadow	2.6 km
Glen Camp	7.4 km
Palomarin	19.0 km
Sky Camp	4.3 km
Wildcat Camp	10.1 km

From Fivebrooks

Wildcat Camp	10.8 km

29. Jeffrey's odometer is not wrong. If Jeffrey rides to Arch Rock and back, he rides twice the distance given the table. The table from Student Activity Sheet 4 suggests that he would have ridden 13.2 kilometers (if you double 6.6 km). However, the first table and the first column of Student Activity Sheet 4 indicate that he actually rode 13,144 meters. This number rounded to one-tenth of a kilometer is 13.1 kilometers, which is the number on Jeffrey's odometer. The difference is caused by rounding errors.

30. Jeffrey did not improve his average speed every day, but his average speed did improve toward the end of the week.

31. 1.3 kilometers per hour

Materials Student Activity Sheet 4 (one per student)

Overview Students round distances given in meters to the nearest kilometer and to the nearest tenth of a kilometer. They solve a problem involving an odometer using their understanding of decimals, measurement, and rounding.

About the Mathematics If all of the digits of a number that represents a measurement are not significant, the unit of measurement can be changed and the number rounded. For example, a distance of 6,601 meters has two *significant digits* (the first and second digits). The unit of measurement can be changed to kilometers (6.601 kilometers) and the number can be rounded to 6.6, or 7 kilometers.

With a calculation involving two decimal numbers, such as adding, if the numbers are rounded first and then added, the answer may be less precise than an answer found by first adding the numbers and then rounding the answer. This is the underlying principle of the problems on this page. It is made more explicit in the Summary on page 82 of the Teacher Guide.

Planning Students can work on problems **26–31** in pairs or in small groups. You may decide to use problem **29** for assessment.

Comments about the Problems

26. In this problem, students must convert meters to kilometers and round the numbers. If students are having difficulty, remind them of the strategy they used to round the populations of the metropolitan areas to the nearest million.

29. Informal Assessment This problem assesses students' understanding of the metric system and its relationship to decimals, and their ability to choose an appropriate visual model or strategy to represent and solve problems involving decimals.

The purpose of this problem is to illustrate that measurement always involves a rounded number.

31. This problem can be solved using a variety of strategies. Have students explain the different strategies they used. Encourage them to reason rather than to use a formal algorithm.

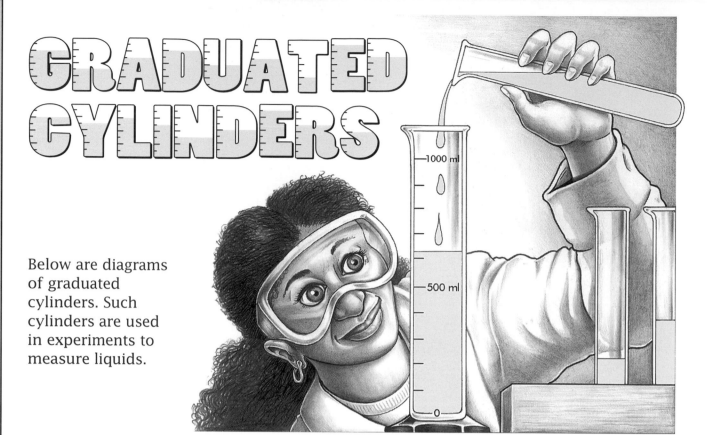

GRADUATED CYLINDERS

Below are diagrams of graduated cylinders. Such cylinders are used in experiments to measure liquids.

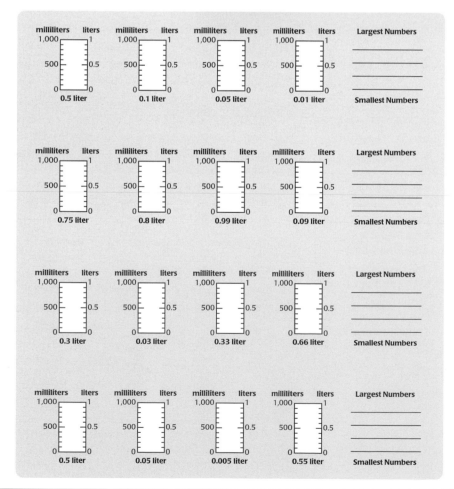

milliliters	liters	milliliters	liters	milliliters	liters	milliliters	liters	Largest Numbers
0.5 liter		0.1 liter		0.05 liter		0.01 liter		Smallest Numbers
0.75 liter		0.8 liter		0.99 liter		0.09 liter		Largest Numbers / Smallest Numbers
0.3 liter		0.03 liter		0.33 liter		0.66 liter		Largest Numbers / Smallest Numbers
0.5 liter		0.05 liter		0.005 liter		0.55 liter		Largest Numbers / Smallest Numbers

32. Look at the cylinders on **Student Activity Sheet 5.** Mark the level of the liquid for each cylinder. Then, for each row, write the amounts—from the largest to the smallest—in the blanks on the right.

33. Which amount in problem **32** was the most difficult to mark? Why?

32.

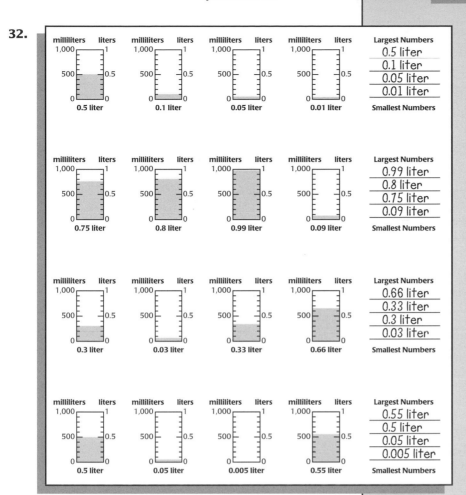

Overview Students mark the levels of liquid in various cylinders and order the amounts from largest to smallest.

About the Mathematics Measuring liquids is the final context in this unit in which students extend their understanding of the metric system. This page introduces the metric units of *liter* and *milliliter*. Explain to students that liter and milliliter measure liquid volume, not length as meters and millimeters do. A milliliter is a refinement of a liter. One milliliter is $\frac{1}{1000}$ of a liter. You may want to bring a one- or two-liter bottle to give students an idea about the volume of such containers. The cylinders pictured on page 80 of the Teacher Guide can be seen as double number lines. The left measurement scale on each cylinder shows milliliters and the right measurement scale shows liters.

33. Answers may vary. Most students will say 0.005 liters was the most difficult to mark because the amount was so small compared to the scale on the cylinder.

Planning Some students may not be familiar with liters. You may want to bring a one- or two-liter bottle to show students. Students can work in pairs on problems **32** and **33.** You can also use problem **32** as an assessment.

Comments about the Problems

32. Informal Assessment This problem assesses students' understanding of place value and its use in ordering decimals, and their understanding of the metric system and its relationship to decimals.

Discuss with students how they determined the order of the numbers. You can ask students: *What do you know about the values of the digits to the right of the decimal point?* [These digits represent $\frac{1}{10}$, $\frac{1}{100}$, or $\frac{1}{1000}$ of one whole.] *Why is five hundredths less than five tenths?* [*Hundredths* means that one whole is divided into 100 equal parts, and *tenths* means that the same whole is divided into 10 equal parts. So, five hundredths is less than five tenths.]

Summary

If a decimal ends with zeros, these "placeholder" zeros can be left off. These zeros are often used to show how precise the measurement is. For example, 0.5 might be the result of rounding, implying that the original number was somewhere between 0.45 and 0.549. If, however, 0.50 was the result of rounding, the ending zero would mean that the original number must have been between 0.495 and 0.5049.

If you round the number 5.657 to 5.7, you are rounding to one *decimal place*. You round up one decimal place to 5.7 instead of down to 5.6 because 5.657 is closer to 5.7 than to 5.6. This is easy to show on a number line.

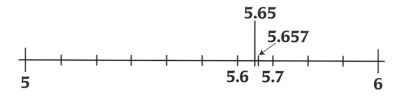

Rounded numbers are easier to read, but can cause measurement errors when combined with other rounded numbers.

For example, think about the numbers 5.5557 and 5.5511:

If you round these numbers to one decimal place first and then add, you have:	If, however, you add the numbers first and then round, you have:
5.6 + 5.6 **11.2**	5.5557 + 5.5511 11.1068 which rounds to **11.1**

Summary Questions

34. a. If 32 is the result of rounding a number, what might the original number have been?

b. If 0.55 is the result of rounding a number, between what two numbers was the original number?

35. How is rounding numbers related to ordering numbers?

34. a. Answers will vary. The original number might have been between 31.49 and 32.5.

   b. Answers will vary. The original number might have been between 0.5449 and 0.555.

35. In both rounding and ordering decimals, you must pay attention to the next digit. For example, to round 2,934,286 to the nearest million, you need to look at the digit to the right of the million's digit (the 9). In this case, the answer is 3 million. To order decimals that are close together, such as 9.53, 9.54, and 9.537, you must look at the hundredths digit to see that 9.54 is the largest number. Then you need to look at the thousandths digit to see that 9.537 is the second largest number.

Overview Students read the Summary, which reviews rounding strategies, such as using a number line. Measurement errors caused by combining rounded numbers are also discussed. Given rounded numbers, students determine the range of possible values for the original number.

Planning Discuss the Summary with the class. You may refer to one of the unit's contexts, such as city populations, to give students a better understanding of rounding numbers. Problem **34** can be used as assessment. After students complete Section D, you may assign appropriate activities from the Try This! section, located on pages 37–40 of the Student Book, as homework.

Comments about the Problems

34. a. Informal Assessment This problem assesses students' understanding of decimals as they relate to refinement in the measurement process.

   Encourage students to use a number line. They need only draw a number line showing 31 to 33. Students then refine this number line. Discuss how to round 31.5, the number halfway between 31 and 32. (Using the conventional method, 31.5 is rounded up to 32.)

Assessment Overview

Students work on three assessments that can be used at the end of the unit. You can evaluate these assessments to determine what each student knows about decimals and which strategies they use to solve each problem.

Goals

- understand the relationship between benchmark fractions and their decimal representations

- use decimals in a context, such as money or measurement

- estimate and compute with decimals

- understand place value and its use in ordering decimals

- understand the metric system and its relationship to decimals

- understand decimals as they relate to refinement in the measurement process

- use equivalent representations of fractions, decimals, and division notation

- represent and use decimals in a variety of equivalent forms to solve problems in real-world and mathematical situations

- choose an appropriate visual model or strategy to represent and solve problems involving decimals

Assessment Opportunities

Penny Tube, problems 1–4

Penny Tube, problems 1 and 2
Metric Units, problem 3
The Bakery, problem 1

Metric Units, problem 3
The Bakery, problems 1 and 2

The Bakery, problem 1

Metric Units, problems 1–3

Metric Units, problem 3

Penny Tube, problems 1–4

Penny Tube, problem 2

Penny Tube, problem 1
Metric Units, problem 3
The Bakery, problems 1 and 2

Pacing

- Approximately one 45-minute class session for all three assessments

About the Mathematics

These end-of-unit activities assess the goals of the *Measure for Measure* unit. Refer to the Goals and Assessment Opportunities section on the previous page for information regarding the goals that are assessed in each activity. The problems do not ask students to use any specific strategy. Students have the option of using any strategy with which they feel comfortable.

Materials

- Assessments, pages 100–102 of this Teacher Guide (one of each per student)
- calculators, pages 100–102 of this Teacher Guide, optional (one per student)

Planning Assessment

You may decide to let students work individually on these assessments if you want to evaluate each student's understanding and abilities. Make sure that you allow enough time for students to complete the assessments. If they need more than one class session, you may assign The Bakery as homework or give additional class time the following day. Students are free to solve the problems in their own ways. Have calculators available for students who want to use them.

Scoring

In scoring the assessment problems, the emphasis should be on the strategies used rather than on students' final answers. Since several strategies can be employed to answer many of the questions, the strategy a student chooses will indicate his or her level of comprehension of the problem and of decimals. For example, a concrete strategy supported by drawings may indicate a deeper understanding than an abstract computational answer. Consider how well students' strategies address the problem, as well as how successful students are at applying their strategies in the problem-solving process.

PENNY TUBE

Use additional paper as needed.

Below you see a penny tube used to collect loose pennies. There is a scale line on the tube to make it easier to count the number of pennies. When the tube is full, it holds 100 pennies. So, a full tube is worth $1.00.

You can describe the contents of a tube in different ways. On this page is a set of fractions. These fractions indicate what part of the tube was filled at different times.

1. **a.** Connect each fraction in the diagram to the appropriate line on the penny tube.

    b. Write the fractions in order from largest to smallest.

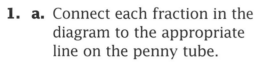

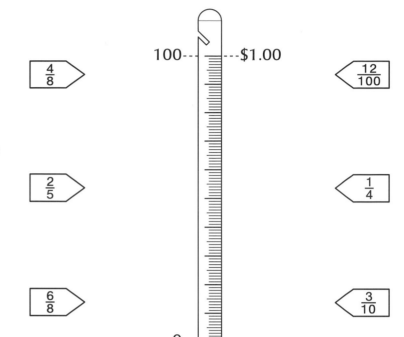

2. Pete could place all but two of the fractions on the penny tube. He did not know where to put $\frac{1}{4}$ or $\frac{6}{8}$. Explain how you placed these fractions on the penny tube.

3. Write these fractions as decimals:

    $\frac{1}{5} =$ $\frac{2}{100} =$

    $\frac{1}{4} =$ $\frac{3}{4} =$

    $\frac{1}{10} =$ $\frac{1}{2} =$

4. Write your four favorite fractions and their decimal equivalents. Why are these your favorite fractions?

Solutions and Samples
of student work

1. a.

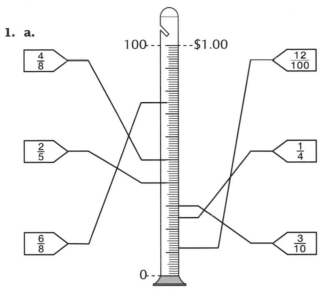

b. $\frac{6}{8}, \frac{4}{5}, \frac{2}{5}, \frac{3}{10}, \frac{1}{4}, \frac{12}{100}$

2. Answers will vary. Possible answers for $\frac{1}{4}$:

I know where $\frac{1}{2}$ of the tube is, and then I figured where $\frac{1}{2}$ of $\frac{1}{2}$ of the tube would be. Since $\frac{1}{2}$ of $\frac{1}{2}$ is $\frac{1}{4}$, I could mark the $\frac{1}{4}$ line.

I thought of $\frac{1}{4}$ as one quarter (the coin) and I know that one quarter is 25 cents. I know that each line represents a penny. So I counted 25 lines.

I know that $\frac{1}{4}$ is equal to 0.25. I marked the 0.25 line.

Possible answers for $\frac{6}{8}$:

I divided the tube into eighths ($\frac{1}{2}$, then $\frac{1}{2}$ of $\frac{1}{2}$ or $\frac{1}{4}$, then $\frac{1}{2}$ of $\frac{1}{4}$) and then counted up to $\frac{6}{8}$.

I used a ratio table and found that $\frac{6}{8}$ was $\frac{3}{4}$. I know that $\frac{3}{4}$ is the same thing as 3 quarters (coins); I counted up 75 lines to represent 3 quarters (75 cents).

I know that $\frac{6}{8}$ is equal to $\frac{3}{4}$, and that $\frac{3}{4}$ is equal to 0.75. I marked the 0.75 line.

3. $\frac{1}{5}$ = 0.20 $\frac{2}{100}$ = 0.02

   $\frac{1}{4}$ = 0.25 $\frac{3}{4}$ = 0.75

   $\frac{1}{10}$ = 0.1 $\frac{1}{2}$ = 0.5 or 0.50

4. Answers will vary. Note which fractions the students choose and why. Some may choose fractions because they know their decimal equivalents. Others may choose certain fractions because they are used often, are larger, or they correspond to money amounts. All of these answers give you some information about the students' familiarity with fractions and their decimal equivalents.

Materials Penny Tube assessment, page 100 of the Teacher Guide (one per student), calculators, optional (one per student)

Overview Students use the divisions (in cents) on the measuring scale of a penny tube to determine where different fractions (of a dollar) belong on the scale. They also convert fractions to decimals.

About the Mathematics These problems assess students' ability to use the relationship between benchmark fractions and their decimal equivalents and to choose an appropriate visual model or strategy to solve problems in which decimals are involved.

Students may use different strategies to solve these problems. They can:
- change the measurement unit from a fraction of a dollar to cents and vice versa,
- use the divisions of the scale to correctly place the fractions and use these results to convert the fractions to decimals, or
- recognize benchmark fractions and their decimal equivalents.

Planning Students may work individually or in pairs on these assessment problems.

Comments about the Problems

1–2. These problems assess students' ability to use decimals in a context.

METRIC UNITS

Use additional paper as needed.

Suppose that a friend of yours does not know much about meters, kilometers, and other metric units of measurement.

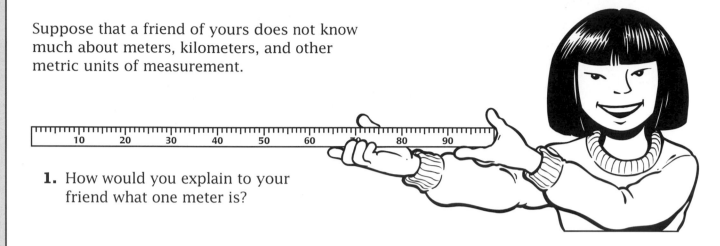

1. How would you explain to your friend what one meter is?

2. How would you explain to your friend what one kilometer is?

At Do-It-Yourself Market, wooden planks cost $2.50 per meter.

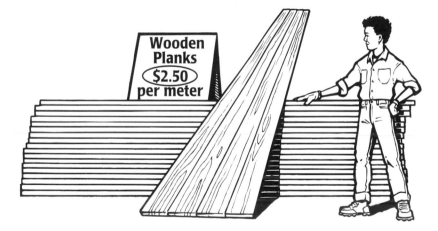

3. Martin buys four wooden planks. Each plank is 2.48 meters long.

   a. Estimate the total length of these planks.

   b. Estimate the amount of money Martin will have to pay.

Solutions and Samples
of student work

1. Answers will vary. Possible responses:

   • One meter is the distance from the bottom of a door to the doorknob.

   • One meter is the distance from the tip of your finger when your arm is stretched out to the tip of your nose.

   • One meter is 100 centimeters, and one centimeter is about the width of your little finger.

2. Answers will vary. Possible responses:

   • One kilometer is the distance of 10 football fields placed end to end.

   • One kilometer is the distance you can walk at a steady pace in about 12 minutes.

   • One kilometer is 1,000 meters.

3. **a.** about 10 meters

   b. Answers will vary. Possible response:

   10 meters × $2.50 = $25.00

Hints and Comments

Materials Metric Units assessment, page 101 of the Teacher Guide (one per student); calculators, optional (one per student)

Overview Students explain the units *meter* and *kilometer* based on their understanding of the metric system and their sense of measurement units.

About the Mathematics These problems assess students' understanding of the metric system and its relationship to decimals. Problem **3** assesses students' understanding of decimals as they relate to refinement in the measurement process. Students must choose an appropriate visual model or strategy to represent and solve this problem.

Planning Students may work individually or in pairs on these assessment problems.

Comments about the Problems

3. Students should realize that a wooden plank with a length of 2.48 meters is about 2.5 meters long. Therefore, the total length of the four planks will be about 10 meters (4 × 2.50 m = 10 m). Then students can multiply 10 meters by $2.50 to estimate the total cost of the four boards (10 × 2.50 = $25). Some students may first compute 4 × $2.50 = $10, and then compute $10 × 2.48 = $24.80 to find the exact total cost.

THE BAKERY

Use additional paper as needed.

The Flour Shop bakery sells cookies, pastries, and muffins. The items are priced as follows:

Large chocolate chip cookie $0.75

Small sugar cookie $0.39

One-dozen donuts $2.05

Large muffin $1.22

1. If you wanted to buy one of everything on this list, how would you estimate the total cost?

Enzo has $5 that he wants to spend in the bakery. He does not have to pay tax on the food, so he can spend the entire amount on cookies, donuts, and muffins. He wants at least two different items from the list above.

2. What can Enzo buy in order to spend as much of his $5 as he can? How much of the $5 will he have left? Explain.

Solutions and Samples
of student work

1. Answers will vary. Focus on how students round numbers and/or pair them.

   Possible answer:

   The price $1.22 is about $1.25, and $0.75 + $1.25 is $2.00. So, $1.22 + $0.75 is about $2.00.

   The price $0.39 is about 40 cents, and $2.05 + $0.40 is $2.45. So, $0.39 + $2.05 is about $2.45.

   The total for all the items would be about $2.00 + $2.45, or about $4.45.

2. The closest possible total is exactly $5.00 (four chocolate chip cookies, one muffin, and two sugar cookies). If students have less than 20 cents left over, however, they should be given credit. Their reasoning is more important than their answer.

   Possible reasoning:

   Enzo can buy five chocolate chip cookies and one muffin. One chocolate chip cookie is $0.75, which is three quarters. Two cookies are six quarters, or $1.50, and three cookies are nine quarters, or $2.25. Four cookies are 12 quarters, or $3.00, and five cookies are 15 quarters, or $3.75. One muffin costs $1.22. So, five chocolate chip cookies and one muffin cost $3.75 + $1.22, or $4.97. He will have three cents left.

   Enzo can buy four chocolate chip cookies that cost a total of $3.00. He can also buy one muffin at $1.22. Now he has spent a total of $3.00 + $1.22 = $4.22. If he buys only these two items, his change will be about $0.80. Or he might decide to buy two sugar cookies, which sell for about $0.40 each. Two sugar cookies would be $0.80 − $0.02 = $0.78. The total cost for the four chocolate chip cookies, one muffin, and two sugar cookies would be $4.22 + $0.78 = $5.00. Enzo would not have any money left.

Materials The Bakery assessment, page 102 of the Teacher Guide (one per student); calculators, optional (one per student)

Overview Students estimate and do simple computation with decimals in the context of buying bakery items.

About the Mathematics These problems assess students' ability to estimate and compute with decimals. Students must choose an appropriate strategy with which to solve the problems. Some students may use the strategy of changing measurement units; they first convert the prices given in dollars to cents. After doing the computation, students must then convert their answer back to dollars.

Planning Students may work individually or in pairs on these assessment problems.

Comments about the Problems

2. Have students explain how they solved this problem. As you listen to students share their strategies, observe the following:
   • how students estimated their totals,
   • how they added the decimals,
   • how they compared their totals to $5,
   • and how they altered the items they chose to get closer to $5.

78%

Measure for Measure
Glossary

The Glossary defines all vocabulary words listed on the Section Opener pages. It includes the mathematical terms that may be new to students, as well as words having to do with the contexts introduced in the unit. (Note: The Student Book has no glossary in order to allow students to construct their own definitions, based on their personal experiences with the unit activities.) The definitions below are specific to the use of the terms in this unit. The page numbers given are from this Teacher Guide.

benchmark fraction (p. 4) a common fraction that is easily recognizable, such as $\frac{1}{4}$ or $\frac{1}{2}$

centimeter (p. 48) a measure of length; there are 100 centimeters in a meter, and there are 10 millimeters in one centimeter

decimal (p. 34) a representation of a fraction in which the denominator is 10, 100, 1,000, and so forth

decimal point (p. 34) the dot that appears in a decimal number

decimeter (p. 48) a measure of length; a decimeter is 10 centimeters; there are 10 decimeters in a meter

double number line (p. 30) a visual model used to represent the equivalencies between two units; for example, a double number line that shows the decimals and their equivalent fractions might display the decimals sequentially along the top of the number line and display the corresponding equivalent fractions along the bottom of the number line.

fraction bar (p. 4) a rectangular visual model subdivided into equal parts that represent the part-whole relationship of a fraction.

kilometer (p. 54) a measure of length; there are 1,000 meters in a kilometer

liter (p. 8) a measure of volume; there are 100 centiliters or 1,000 milliliters in 1 liter

meter (p. 48) a measure of length; there are 10 decimeters, 100 centimeters, or 1,000 millimeters in one meter

milliliter (p. 80) a measure of volume; a milliliter is one-thousandth of a liter

millimeter (p. 50) a measure of length; there are 1,000 millimeters in one meter

number line (p. 44) a vertical or horizontal line with numbers that can be used as a scale to find distances between numbers

precision in measurement (p. 4) measurements can be refined by subdividing the unit of measure into smaller equal parts. For example, the measurement unit *centimeter* can be subdivided into 10 equal parts called *millimeters*. Measuring to the nearest millimeter is more precise than measuring to the nearest centimeter

rounding (p. 58) to express a number to the nearest million, thousand, one, tenth, hundredth, and so on

significant digits (p. 79) the digits one through nine are always significant when reporting measures. The digit zero is not significant unless it is used to indicate that a measurement is found to be zero. For example, in the measurement 0.075 meter, the digits seven and five are significant. The zeros are used only as placeholders and therefore are not significant.

Blackline Masters

Dear Family,

Your child is about to begin working on the *Mathematics in Context* unit *Measure for Measure*. Below is a letter to your child, describing the unit and its goals.

You can help your child relate the class work to his or her own life by talking about decimals as you encounter them. For instance, you might have your child calculate the total cost of items when you go to stores or restaurants. Have your child round the prices of several items to the nearest dime, quarter, half-dollar, or dollar. Ask your child to order the items on a grocery receipt from least to most expensive.

Spend some time looking at the odometer in a car. When you pump gas into your car, have your child pay attention to the dials that register the amount of gas delivered and the total cost. Explain the $\frac{9}{10}$ that gas stations use to advertise the prices at their pumps.

Enjoy helping your child begin to explore decimals, fractions, and measurement.

Dear Student,

Welcome to *Measure for Measure*.

Throughout this unit, you will study concepts related to decimals. You will study the relationship between fractions and decimals, decimal place value, rounding, estimating, and ordering decimals. You will be introduced to informal strategies for simple computations, decimal number sense, and metric units of measure.

Having worked with money in everyday situations, you already know a lot about decimals. This unit will encourage you to explore and add to what you already know.

You will be investigating the ancient Egyptian number systems, calculating combinations of coins in order to purchase items, ranking singers in an amateur talent show, estimating the number of pennies in a collection tube, ordering and rounding population numbers, and measuring distances and speeds for bike trails in a park.

By the end of this unit, you will have begun to understand decimals and be able to use them in a variety of everyday situations. This knowledge will be important to you throughout your life and will help you in your study of units to come.

Sincerely,

The Mathematics in Context Development Team

Sincerely,

The Mathematics in Context Development Team

17. Write fractions for the symbols in the table below. The first one has been done for you.

Number of 1's	Number of $\frac{1}{10}$'s	Number of $\frac{1}{100}$'s	Number of $\frac{1}{1000}$'s	Number Expression (1's $+ \frac{1}{10}$'s $+ \frac{1}{100}$'s $+ \frac{1}{1000}$'s)
0	3	1	0	$\frac{3}{10} + \frac{1}{100}$

a. ‒ ‒ ‒ ‒ ⌡

b. ‒ ‒ ‒ ‒ ‒ ‒

c. ⌡ ⌡ ⌡ ⌡

d. Ω ‒ ‒ ‒ ⌡⌡

e. ⌡⌡⌡⌡⌡⌡

f. ⌡ ‒ ‒ ‒ ‒ ⌡⌡ ⌡⌡⌡

g. ‒ ‒ ℧℧ ℧℧

Use with *Measure for Measure*, page 17.

16. Use your calculator and your number sense to complete the table below.

Division	Decimal	Fraction
6 ÷ 12		
	0.25	
		$\frac{7}{10}$
		$\frac{1}{8}$
3 ÷ 4		
	0.1	
		$\frac{2}{5}$

21. Round each population to the nearest million. Atlanta and Indianapolis have been done for you.

City	Population	Population (to the nearest million)
Atlanta	2,959,950	3
Baltimore	2,382,172	
Boston	5,455,403	
Buffalo	1,189,288	
Chicago	8,239,820	
Cincinnati	1,817,571	
Cleveland	2,859,644	
Dallas	4,037,282	
Denver	1,980,140	
Detroit	5,187,171	
Houston	3,731,131	
Indianapolis	1,380,491	1
Kansas City, MO	1,582,875	
Los Angeles	14,531,529	
Miami	3,192,582	
Milwaukee	1,607,183	
New Orleans	1,285,270	
New York City	19,549,649	
Orlando	1,224,852	
Philadelphia	5,892,937	
Pittsburgh	2,394,811	
Portland, OR	1,793,476	
St. Louis, MO	2,492,525	
San Antonio	1,324,749	
San Diego	2,498,016	
San Francisco	6,253,311	
Seattle	2,970,328	
Washington, D.C.	4,223,485	

Name _____

Use with *Measure for Measure*, page 34.

27. Round each distance to the nearest kilometer.

From Bear Valley (one way):	Meters	Kilometers	Nearest Tenth of a Kilometer
Arch Rock	6,572 m	7 km	6.6 km
Coast Camp	9,338 m		
Divide Meadow	2,576 m		
Glen Camp	7,406 m		
Palomarin	18,998 m		
Sky Camp	4,347 m		
Wildcat Camp	10,143 m		
From Fivebrooks (one way):	Meters	Kilometers	Nearest Tenth of a Kilometer
Wildcat Camp	10,787 m		

28. Round each distance to the nearest tenth of a kilometer. Explain how you got your answers.

32. Mark the level of the liquid for each cylinder. Then, for each row, write the amounts—from the largest to the smallest—in the blanks on the right.

milliliters	liters	milliliters	liters	milliliters	liters	milliliters	liters	**Largest Numbers**

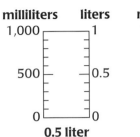 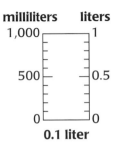 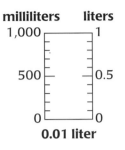 

0.5 liter   0.1 liter   0.05 liter   0.01 liter   **Smallest Numbers**

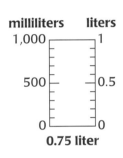 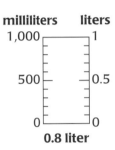 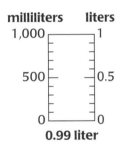 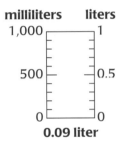 

0.75 liter   0.8 liter   0.99 liter   0.09 liter   **Largest Numbers** / **Smallest Numbers**

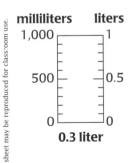 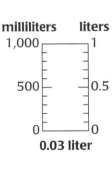 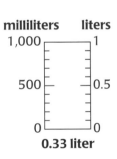 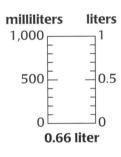 

0.3 liter   0.03 liter   0.33 liter   0.66 liter   **Largest Numbers** / **Smallest Numbers**

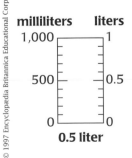 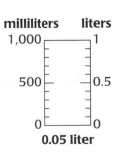 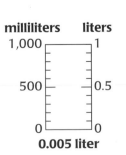 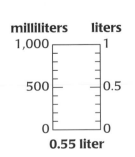

0.5 liter   0.05 liter   0.005 liter   0.55 liter   **Largest Numbers** / **Smallest Numbers**

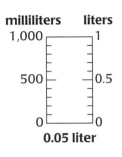

PENNY TUBE

Use additional paper as needed.

Below you see a penny tube used to collect loose pennies. There is a scale line on the tube to make it easier to count the number of pennies. When the tube is full, it holds 100 pennies. So, a full tube is worth $1.00.

You can describe the contents of a tube in different ways. On this page is a set of fractions. These fractions indicate what part of the tube was filled at different times.

1. **a.** Connect each fraction in the diagram to the appropriate line on the penny tube.

   b. Write the fractions in order from largest to smallest.

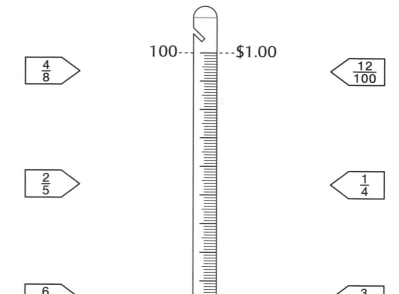

2. Pete could place all but two of the fractions on the penny tube. He did not know where to put $\frac{1}{4}$ or $\frac{6}{8}$. Explain how you placed these fractions on the penny tube.

3. Write these fractions as decimals:

   $\frac{1}{5}$ = $\frac{2}{100}$ =

   $\frac{1}{4}$ = $\frac{3}{4}$ =

   $\frac{1}{10}$ = $\frac{1}{2}$ =

4. Write your four favorite fractions and their decimal equivalents. Why are these your favorite fractions?

METRIC UNITS

Use additional paper as needed.

Suppose that a friend of yours does not know much about meters, kilometers, and other metric units of measurement.

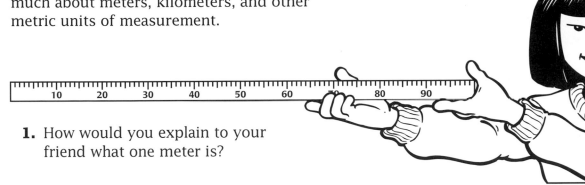

1. How would you explain to your friend what one meter is?

2. How would you explain to your friend what one kilometer is?

At Do-It-Yourself Market, wooden planks cost $2.50 per meter.

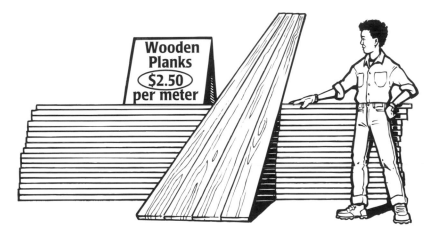

3. Martin buys four wooden planks. Each plank is 2.48 meters long.

a. Estimate the total length of these planks.

b. Estimate the amount of money Martin will have to pay.

THE BAKERY

Use additional paper as needed.

The Flour Shop bakery sells cookies, pastries, and muffins. The items are priced as follows:

Large chocolate chip cookie	$0.75
Small sugar cookie	$0.39
One-dozen donuts	$2.05
Large muffin	$1.22

1. If you wanted to buy one of each item on this list, how would you estimate the total cost?

Enzo has $5 that he wants to spend in the bakery. He does not have to pay tax on the food, so he can spend the entire amount on cookies, donuts, and muffins. He wants at least two different items from the list above.

2. What can Enzo buy in order to spend as much of his $5 as possible? How much of the $5 will he have left? Explain.

Section A. On Being Precise

1. a. 1

   b. $\frac{7}{8}$

   c. $\frac{11}{16}$

2. a. $\frac{1}{4}$;

   b. $\frac{1}{8}$;

   c. $\frac{7}{8}$;

3. a–d.

$\frac{1}{2}$	$\frac{1}{4}$	$\frac{1}{8}$	$\frac{1}{16}$	

4. Answers will vary. Students will express their answers using varying degrees of precision (to the nearest whole strip, one-half strip, one-fourth strip, or one-eighth strip).

Section B. It Just Makes Cents

1. a. Estimates will vary. Sample estimates:
Marcia: $27.00; Annette: $27.00

b. Answers will vary. It is probably not clear to most students who collected more money. Explanations will vary but should indicate the fact that since the estimates for both girls were almost or exactly equal, a more precise method is needed to find out which girl collected the most money, such as an exact computation or more precise estimation.

c. Marcia collected $26.70.

d. Annette collected $26.94.

e. Answers will vary. Some students may say that using a calculator would be faster; others might suggest that it is faster to look for patterns in the numbers and combine cent amounts that add up to one dollar.

2.

Division	Decimal	Fraction
$6 \div 10$	0.60	$\frac{6}{10}$ or $\frac{3}{5}$
$4 \div 10$	0.40	$\frac{4}{10}$ or $\frac{2}{5}$
$8 \div 10$	0.80	$\frac{8}{10}$ or $\frac{4}{5}$
$7 \div 14$	0.50	$\frac{7}{14}$ or $\frac{1}{2}$
$2 \div 10$	0.20	$\frac{2}{10}$ or $\frac{1}{5}$
$3 \div 10$	0.30	$\frac{3}{10}$
$3 \div 8$	0.375	$\frac{3}{8}$

3. a. $\frac{3}{5} + \frac{5}{10} = 0.60 + 0.50 = 1.10 = 1\frac{1}{10}$

b. $\frac{3}{10} + \frac{1}{5} = 0.30 + 0.20 = 0.50 = \frac{1}{2}$

c. $\frac{1}{2} + \frac{1}{4} = 0.50 + 0.25 = 0.75 = \frac{3}{4}$

d. $\frac{1}{4} + \frac{1}{4} = 0.25 + 0.25 = 0.50 = \frac{1}{2}$

Section C. Sporting Decimals

1. **a.** 2,200 centimeters

   b. 7 meters

   c. 240 millimeters

   d. 40 kilometers

2. Answers will vary. Sample answers:

   a. 235.4 centimeters; 2.354 meters; $23\frac{54}{100}$ decimeters; about 23 and one-half decimeters; between 23 and 24 decimeters

   b. 20,000 centimeters; 2,000 decimeters; 200,000 millimeters

   c. $34\frac{98}{100}$ millimeters; $34 + \frac{9}{10} + \frac{8}{100}$ millimeters; just under 35 millimeters; 3.498 centimeters; 0.3498 decimeters

   d. 100 millimeters; 1 decimeter; or 0.10 meter

   e. 833 centimeters; 83.3 decimeters; $8 + \frac{3}{10} + \frac{3}{100}$ meters

3. Answers will vary. Sample answers:

   a. $34\frac{56}{100}$ seconds; $34 + \frac{5}{10} + \frac{6}{100}$ seconds; $34\frac{28}{50}$ seconds

   b. $8\frac{8}{100}$ seconds; $8\frac{4}{50}$ seconds; eight and eight-hundredths seconds

   c. $425\frac{7}{100}$ miles; $425 + \frac{0}{10} + \frac{7}{100}$ miles; four hundred twenty-five and seven hundredths miles

   d. $\frac{5}{100}$ meter; five-hundredths of a meter; $\frac{1}{20}$ meter

4. Answers will vary. Sample answers:

   a. A pencil or pen is about 15 centimeters long.

   b. A tall man is about 2 meters tall.

   c. The width of a tennis court is about 10 meters long.

   d. A doorknob is about 1 meter from the bottom of the door.

Section D. Ordering Decimals

1. Answers will vary. Refer to the glossary on page 92 of this Teacher Guide.

2. Estimates will vary. Sample estimates:

    a. $9.00   **b.** $9.00   **c.** $15.00   **d.** $9.00

3. a. 0.075, 0.75, 7.057, 7.5, 7.57, 75.7

   b. 0.00883, 0.0883, 0.883, 8.83, 88.3

   c. 0.0564, 0.564, 5.64, 56.4, 564, 5,640

   d. 0.76, 0.80, 6.76, 6.82, 68.2, 78.3

4. a. Nadia

   b.

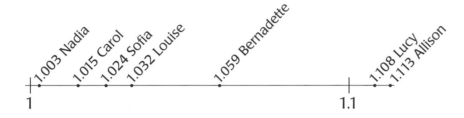

   c. 1.086 minutes

   d. Nadia, Carol, and Sofia

Cover

Design by Ralph Paquet/Encyclopædia Britannica Educational Corporation

Collage by Koorosh Jamalpur/KJ Graphics

Title Page

Illustration by Paul Tucker/Encyclopædia Britannica Educational Corporation

Illustrations

6, 8, 10 Paul Tucker/Encyclopædia Britannica Educational Corporation; **12 (bottom)** Phil Geib/Encyclopædia Britannica Educational Corporation; **12 (top), 14** Brent Cardillo/Encyclopædia Britannica Educational Corporation; **16** Paul Tucker/Encyclopædia Britannica Educational Corporation; **20** Jerome Gordon; **22, 24** Phil Geib/Encyclopædia Britannica Educational Corporation; **26, 30** Jerome Gordon; **32** Phil Geib/Encyclopædia Britannica Educational Corporation; **34** Paul Tucker/Encyclopædia Britannica Educational Corporation; **38 (bottom), 40, 42, 44, 46, 56, 58, 60, 62, 64, 74, 76, 78** Phil Geib/Encyclopædia Britannica Educational Corporation; **82** Jerome Gordon; **84** Brent Cardillo/Encyclopædia Britannica Educational Corporation; **86** Paul Tucker/Encyclopædia Britannica Educational Corporation; **90** Paul Tucker/Encyclopædia Britannica Educational Corporation; **92, 94** Phil Geib/Encyclopædia Britannica Educational Corporation

Photographs

34 © David Alexovich/Encyclopædia Britannica Educational Corporation